Get Started
Knitting

Get Started

Knitting

DK

LONDON, NEW YORK, MUNICH,
MELBOURNE, DELHI

Project Editor Becky Shackleton
Project Art Editor Gemma Fletcher
Senior Editor Alastair Laing
Managing Editor Penny Warren
Managing Art Editor Alison Donovan
Senior Jacket Creative Nicola Powling
Jacket Design Assistant Rosie Levine
Pre-production Producer Sarah Isle
Senior Producers Seyhan Esen, Jen Lockwood
Art Directors Peter Luff, Jane Bull
Publisher Mary Ling

DK Publishing

North American Consultant Jenn Wendell
Editor Jane Perlmutter
Senior Editor Shannon Beatty

DK India

Art Editors Ranjita Bhattacharji, Tanya Mehrotra
Senior Art Editor Ivy Roy
Managing Editor Alka Thakur Hazarika
Deputy Managing Art Editor Priyabrata Roy Chowdhury

Written by Susie Johns

First American Edition, 2013

Published in the United States by DK Publishing,
375 Hudson Street, New York, New York 10014

13 14 15 16 17 10 9 8 7 6 5 4 3 2 1
001—187849—Jan/2013

Published in Great Britain by Dorling Kindersley Limited.

A catalog record for this book is available from the
Library of Congress.

ISBN 978-1-4654-0197-7

DK books are available at special discounts when purchased in
bulk for sales promotions, premiums, fund-raising, or educational
use. For details, contact: DK Publishing Special Markets, 375
Hudson Street, New York, New York 10014 or
SpecialSales@dk.com.

Printed and bound by Leo Paper Products Ltd, China

Discover more at
www.dk.com

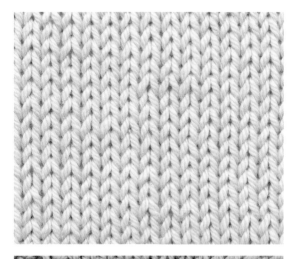

Contents

1

Start Simple

2

Build On It

3

Take It Further

Build Your Course

This book is divided into three sections: Start Simple, Build On It, and Take It Further. These chapters are carefully structured to help you learn new skills and techniques and then cement your increasing knowledge by completing the step-by-step projects.

Key Techniques

Close-up images show you exactly what you need to do

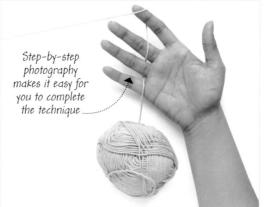

Step-by-step photography makes it easy for you to complete the technique

Annotation picks out important details

The key techniques show you everything you need to know to complete your knitting projects easily and successfully, and appear immediately before the projects they are needed for. They range from simple skills such as holding your needles correctly and casting on, to advanced techniques such as creating textures and using color patterns. The step-by-step photography and detailed annotation will help you practice these skills before you attempt a project, and the helpful tips will help you avoid mistakes.

Patterns

Your knitting pattern is your stitch-by-stitch key to constructing your project, so it's vital that you understand it. You'll build up your knowledge and familiarity of the abbreviations gradually, but refer to the chart on pp.26–27.

Heart Motif

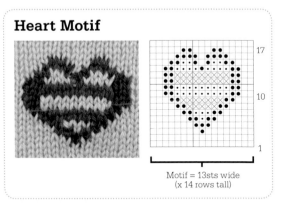

Motif = 13sts wide
(x 14 rows tall)

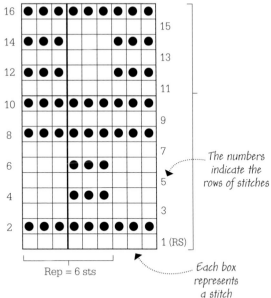

The numbers indicate the rows of stitches

Rep = 6 sts

Each box represents a stitch

The perfect **Project**

After the pattern, each project is assessed and annotated, with the most difficult elements discussed in detail so that you can see exactly what your finished project should look like.

Annotation highlights key stitchings and other details

The key features of your item are flagged

Key Details

These useful illustrated boxes pick out the defining features of your project and explain how to achieve them, giving tips and advice to help you pull off a professional finish.

Knitting Needles

STRAIGHT NEEDLES

A pair of straight needles is the conventional choice and a good place to begin when you are starting to knit. Needles come in various lengths, to accommodate different widths of knitting, and a range of thicknesses to suit different weights of yarn. They are made from a range of different materials, including wood, metal, and plastic, each of which has its own benefits.

Plastic needles
Plastic is lightweight and remains at a steady temperature; it is also relatively cheap. Avoid plastic needles of US6 (4mm/UK8) or smaller, however, because heavy fabrics may bend or break them.

Bamboo needles
Lightweight and flexible, these needles help to keep stitches evenly spaced, creating an even tension. Bamboo is a good choice for slippery yarns such as silk and mercerized cotton.

Metal needles
A good choice for knitters who tend to knit too tightly—the slippery metal surface can help to loosen the tension. Because they are quite heavy, metal needles are rarely available in larger sizes.

Ebony and rosewood needles
Expensive to buy, wood needles have a waxy surface when new, and feel quite luxurious to work with. Like bamboo, they help to create an even tension.

Square needles
While most needles are rounded in shape, this relatively new innovation has a faceted surface and a pointed tip, which helps to relieve stress on the hands, making this type of needle particularly suitable for people with arthritis.

Cable needles
Short, straight or kinked double-pointed needles are used to hold stitches waiting to be knit in cable patterns. The kinked shape helps to prevent stitches from slipping off the needle.

Needle sizes
Knitting needles vary in diameter from ¹/₁₆in (1.5mm) to over 1in (2.5cm). There are three different sizing systems in use: in the UK, the previous system has been replaced by European metric measurements, while the United States has its own sizing system.

Conversion chart

This chart shows the approximate equivalents for the three different sizing systems in operation. For knitting needles that do not have a size marked, use a needle gauge (see p.20) to measure them.

EU Metric	Old UK	US
1.5mm	N/A	000/00
2mm	14	0
2.25mm/2.5mm	13	1
2.75mm	12	2
3mm	11	N/A
3.25mm	10	3
3.5mm	N/A	4
3.75mm	9	5
4mm	8	6
4.5mm	7	7
5mm	6	8
5.5mm	5	9
6mm	4	10
6.5mm	3	10½
7mm	2	N/A
7.5mm	1	N/A
8mm	0	11
9mm	00	13
10mm	000	15
12mm	N/A	17
15mm	N/A	19
20mm	N/A	35
25mm	N/A	50

DOUBLE-POINTED AND CIRCULAR NEEDLES

Circular needles and sets of double-pointed needles will increase your versatility as a knitter. Both types can be used to produce a tube of seamless knitting, but while circular needles are invaluable for larger items such as sweaters, most are too long for knitting small projects like socks and gloves. Double-pointed needles also tend to be quite short, so they will not accommodate a large number of stitches.

Double-pointed metal needles
Metal is the traditional choice, but since it tends to be heavier than other materials, these are available mainly in smaller sizes.

Double-pointed bamboo needles
Bamboo is light in weight, less slippery than metal, comfortable to hold, and a popular choice with modern knitters.

Double-pointed plastic needles
Plastic needles are lightweight, but liable to snap. They are, however, much cheaper to buy for knitters on a budget.

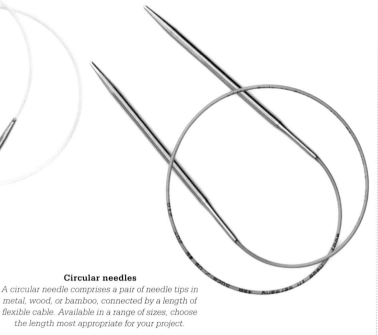

Circular needles
A circular needle comprises a pair of needle tips in metal, wood, or bamboo, connected by a length of flexible cable. Available in a range of sizes, choose the length most appropriate for your project.

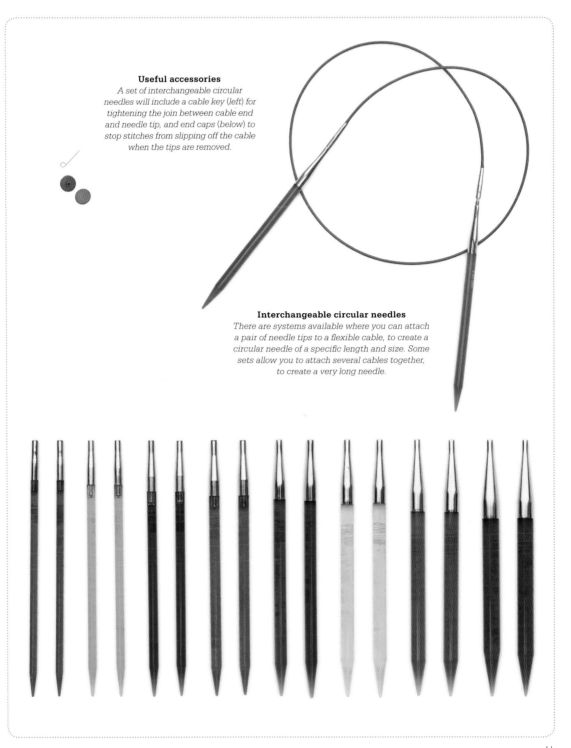

Useful accessories

A set of interchangeable circular needles will include a cable key (left) for tightening the join between cable end and needle tip, and end caps (below) to stop stitches from slipping off the cable when the tips are removed.

Interchangeable circular needles

There are systems available where you can attach a pair of needle tips to a flexible cable, to create a circular needle of a specific length and size. Some sets allow you to attach several cables together, to create a very long needle.

Essential **Yarns**

NATURAL FIBERS

Yarns are spun from fibers, many of which come from sources in nature, including animal hair and plant fibers. A yarn might be created from a single fiber or from several fibers blended together, to make the most of certain attributes such as strength, softness, and elasticity.

Wool

Fleece from sheep is made into pure-wool yarns or blended with other fibers. Some wool fibers can be quite rough, but will soften with wear. Wool is very warm and hard-wearing, and is therefore ideal for winter sweaters, jackets, hats, and gloves.

Alpaca

A relative of the llama, the alpaca provides one of the warmest natural fibers with a soft, luxurious feel. Alpaca yarns have good insulating properties and are, therefore, perfect for items of winter wear such as ski hats, cozy sweaters, and socks.

Silk

The silk worm spins a cocoon in order to develop into a moth and it is from these fibers that silk is made. Silk yarns can be expensive to buy, but silk blends are more affordable and are perfect for baby clothes and special-occasion wear.

Cotton

This plant fiber produces hard-wearing yarns that are naturally matte in appearance, but can be treated (mercerized) to give them an attractive sheen. Fabrics knit from cotton yarns hold their shape well, so are particularly good for homewares and bags.

Cashmere

Spun from a certain type of goat hair, cashmere yarns are soft and luxurious. Cashmere is light but very strong and is often blended with other fibers to add softness. Enjoy cashmere close to your skin by knitting it into scarves and sweaters.

Mohair

Spun from the hair of a furry breed of goat, mohair yarns are very fuzzy and challenging to knit with because the stitches can be difficult to see. Use it for oversized sweaters and shawls, but not for baby clothes since it tends to shed its fibers.

SYNTHETIC FIBERS AND YARN BLENDS

Man-made fibers can be made to resemble their natural counterparts or created to add strength or reduce bulk when blended with other fibers. Synthetics also offer a variety of interesting textures not found in nature. Although they do not hold warmth, they can be washed at high temperatures and tumble-dried.

Microfiber
Increasingly common in multifiber blends, across the range from budget to luxury yarns, microfiber helps to hold the other fibers in the blend together and reduces the density, creating lightweight yarns that are less likely to "pill" or become felted.

Acrylic
Produced from a by-product of petrochemicals, acrylic yarns are cheap to manufacture. Acrylics can have a rougher texture than other synthetics, but are very hard-wearing, resistant to moths, and can be dyed in bright colors.

Nylon
Otherwise known as "polyamide," nylon is very strong, lightweight, and elastic. It is often added to yarn blends for making socks, to add strength, improve washability, and prevent shrinkage and felting.

Wool and cotton blends
While wool is warm, it can be scratchy, so the strength and softness of cotton adds smoothness, breathability, and washability—and makes perfect yarns for knitting clothes for babies and people with sensitive skins.

Natural and synthetic mixes
When man-made fibers are added to natural fibers, they help to create structure, strength, and washability. They can also change the appearance of a natural yarn, adding a sheen.

Synthetic-only mixes
Yarn manufacturers mix synthetic fibers to create interesting textures, such as soft, smooth yarns for baby knits. Synthetic yarns are not as warm as natural fibers, but they can be machine washed at high temperatures.

SPECIALITY YARNS

When it comes to adding texture or sparkle to knitting, there are some very interesting yarns available, with manufacturers continuing to come up with new and exciting innovations. If you like to experiment, shop around and you will find a wealth of different yarns, both natural and synthetic, to add special effects to your knit fabrics, encouraging creativity.

Slubby yarn
Often hand spun from natural fibers such as wool and cotton, these yarns vary in thickness along the length of the strands, creating an uneven, lumpy fabric when knit, which can be good for outer garments, hats, cushions, and throws.

Spun yarn
Very thick yarns, when loosely spun, are less dense than regular yarns, and are light and bouncy. These chunky yarns are intended to prevent finished items from feeling heavy and are ideal for knitting bulky cardigans, blankets, and baby-carriage covers.

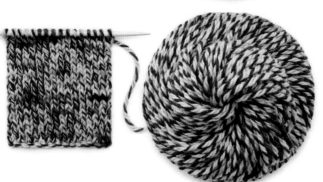

Plied yarn
A plied yarn is made up of two or more strands of spun fiber twisted together. Originally, the number of "plies" defined a yarn's thickness, but these days many plied yarns vary in weight and are likely to contain several colors.

Tweed yarn
Tweeds were once made from a mixture of undyed, natural light and dark wool, to create a flecked appearance. These days, tweed yarns are spun in a variety of colors, from subtle to bright, but are always distinguished by the flecked pattern.

Bouclé yarn
The curly appearance results from loops of fiber attached to a solid core of yarn. When knit, the loops create a thick fabric, reminiscent of a sheep's fleece. Bouclé yarns are a good choice for thick, winter cardigans and jackets and for warm, stylish throws.

Eyelash yarn
The tufted appearance of this family of yarns is created by attaching lengths of various materials to a solid core of yarn. These novelty yarns are popular for making scarves and children's clothes and are an excellent choice for trims and edgings.

YARN WEIGHT CHART

Yarns are available in a range of weights and thicknesses. Important information —yarn weight, recommended needle size, and gauge—is usually printed on the yarn's ball band. Use this information to select the best yarn for your project.

What Do You Want To Knit?	Yarn Weight	Yarn Symbol	Recommended Needle Sizes		
			METRIC	US	OLD UK
Lace	fingering-ply, lace,	0 Lace	2mm 2.5mm	0 1	14 13
Fine-knit socks, shawls, baby clothes	Sock, fingerling 3-ply, superfine, baby	1 Super-fine	2.75mm 3mm 3.25mm	2 N/A 3	12 11 10
Light sweaters, baby clothes, socks, accessories	sport-ply, fine, baby	2 Fine	3.5mm 3.75mm 4mm	4 5 6	N/A 9 8
Sweaters, lightweight scarves, blankets, toys	Double knit (DK), light worsted, 5–6 ply	3 Light	4.5mm	7	7
Sweaters, cabled menswear, blankets, hats, scarves, mittens	aran, medium, Afghan, 12-ply	4 Medium	5mm 5.5mm	8 9	6 5
Rugs, jackets, blankets, hats, leg warmers, winter accessories	Chunky, bulky, craft, rug, 14-ply	5 Bulky	6mm 6.5mm 7mm 8mm	10 10½ N/A 11	4 3 2 0
Heavy blankets, rugs, thick scarves	super bulky, super chunky, roving, 16-ply and upward	6 Super bulky	9mm 10mm	13 15	00 000

KNITTING WITH DIFFERENT WEIGHTS OF YARN

Select the most suitable weight of yarn and the correct size needles for your project. The samples shown here indicate what various weights of yarn look like when knit in stockinette stitch. In each case, the yarn weight names give the common US term(s) followed by the equivalent UK term(s).

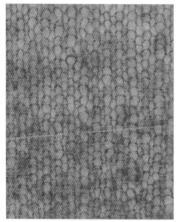

Fingering

Perfect for knitting lace, a ball of this yarn goes a long way. Using very thin needles, superfine yarns highlight fine detail and stitch definition. They are the classic choice for newborn baby clothes.

Sport

This weight produces fine knit fabrics, ideal for baby clothes and socks. It is also a good choice for slim-fitting sweaters that use delicate stitch textures or colorwork such as traditional Fair Isle patterns.

Double-Knit (DK)/
Light Worsted/5–6 PLY

Probably the most popular weight, DK is useful for all kinds of knits, from blankets and sweaters to toys and accessories. It knits up more quickly than sport and produces a medium-weight fabric.

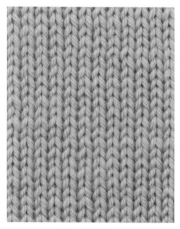

Worsted/Aran

This yarn is the traditional choice for cable knits. With the correct needles (see chart opposite), it produces a fabric that is soft and not too heavy. Worsted yarns are available in wool, as well as mixed, fibers.

Chunky/Bulky

Though chunky yarns are thick and bulky, they are often composed of lightweight fibers to avoid knit garments being too heavy and drooping out of shape. Use them for thick jackets, hats, and scarves.

Super bulky/
Extra bulky

These yarns vary in thickness, but always require large needles. Popular with many beginners because they knit up quickly, use these extra-thick "statement" yarns for making rugged hats and scarves.

Essential **Equipment**

There are hundreds of different tools and gadgets available to knitters, with new innovations coming onto the market all the time. Before you get carried away and buy more than you need, here is a guide to the absolute essentials you will need to start knitting. These basic items are relatively inexpensive and easily available from haberdashery stores and knitting suppliers, either in person or online. To save money, shop around: some items, such as stitch holders and gauges, can be found secondhand, in flea markets and charity stores, or passed down from family members.

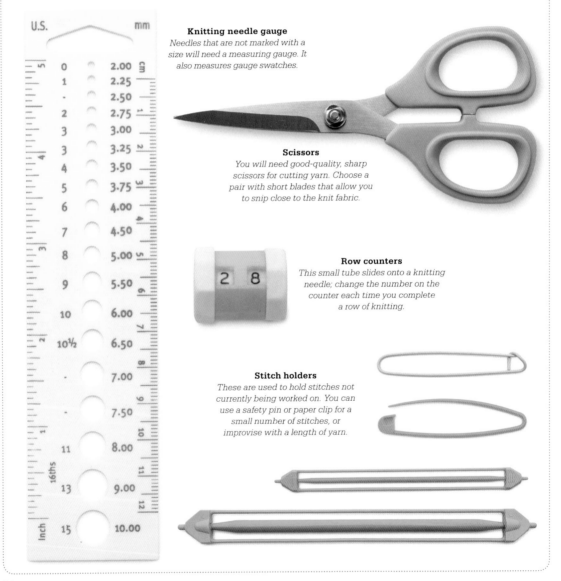

Knitting needle gauge
Needles that are not marked with a size will need a measuring gauge. It also measures gauge swatches.

Scissors
You will need good-quality, sharp scissors for cutting yarn. Choose a pair with short blades that allow you to snip close to the knit fabric.

Row counters
This small tube slides onto a knitting needle; change the number on the counter each time you complete a row of knitting.

Stitch holders
These are used to hold stitches not currently being worked on. You can use a safety pin or paper clip for a small number of stitches, or improvise with a length of yarn.

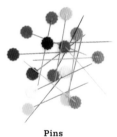

Pins
Choose pins with large heads that are less likely to get lost in the gaps between stitches. Use them to pin pieces of knitting together before sewing up and to pin out work when blocking (see p.141).

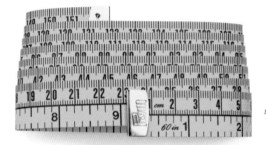

Tape measure
Use this to measure the person you are knitting for, and for work in progress. For measuring tension, a ruler is more accurate.

Stitch markers
Use these to mark the beginning and end of an area of work or to identify the end of a round when working on a circular knitting pin or set of double-pointed needles.

Knitting bag
Choose a bag made from a firm, lightweight fabric, with pockets for small items and a large central compartment to accommodate your current project.

Needle organizer
A specially designed wallet with narrow pockets will keep needles organized and protect them from damage. If you can sew, why not make a customized organizer to suit your own needs?

Knitting beads and buttons
You will need buttons for closing up certain garments, and it is handy to have a selection of different shapes and colors in your knitting bag. Beads are not absolutely essential, but any creative knitter will find dozens of uses for them.

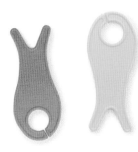

Yarn bobbins

*When using a small amount of yarn
—in intarsia knitting, for
example—wind yarn onto bobbins
to prevent them from becoming
tangled.*

Point protectors

*Put these rubber caps onto needle tips
to stop stitches from sliding off when
not in use. They also protect needle
tips from damage and stop them from
puncturing your knitting bag.*

Shaped needles

*You may find that a large, blunt needle
with a kinked tip helps to speed up
the sewing process by resurfacing
along the seam more quickly and
efficiently than a straight needle.*

Crochet hook

*These make easy work
of picking up dropped
stitches and can also be
used for inserting bundles
of thread when making
fringes and tassels.*

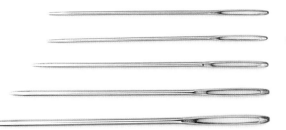

Blunt-ended yarn needles

*To sew up projects, a blunt
(tapestry) needle is better than
a sharp (darning) needle,
because it is less likely to
damage delicate yarn fibers.
You will need a selection
of large-eyed needles of
various sizes for different
thicknesses of yarn.*

Choosing Colors

YARN COLORS

Color is an important consideration, affecting the appearance of a finished item dramatically, so choose your yarns with care: warm or cool colors, pastels, brights, or naturals. The color wheel—made up of all the colors in the spectrum—can be a useful tool when choosing color combinations.

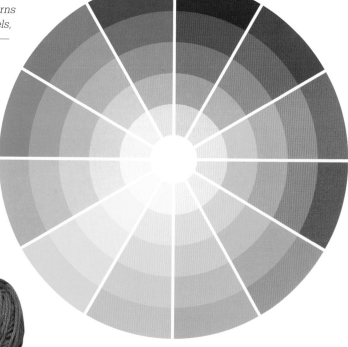

Using a color wheel
Refer to this to see how colors work together. Colors on opposite sides of the wheel—red and green, for example, or yellow and violet—complement each other and provide a contrast, while colors that lie side by side harmonize with each other.

Warm shades
The warm end of the spectrum encompasses reds, oranges, yellows, and red-violet. These colors provide richness as well as brightness. A blend of warm shades can be very flattering.

Black and white
Black and white do not appear on the color wheel, since they are not classified as colors. Black yarn does not show cables and textured stitches to best effect and can be difficult and tiring to work with, because stitches are more difficult to see. White yarns show the subtleties of stitch patterns, but they also show dirty marks and need to be washed more frequently.

Pastels

Pale colors are very popular for baby clothes and also tend to feature in pattern collections for spring and summer garments. It is easy to combine a number of pastel shades harmoniously.

Brights

Vivid shades are popular for children's knits and will appeal to knitters who like to make a strong statement. If you are not confident about combining several bright colors, it may be easier to stick with a single color—or try pairing two bright shades for eye-catching striped sweaters or accessories.

Cool shades

Blues, greens, and violets are at the cool end of the spectrum and are typically darker in tone than warm shades. Hold different colored balls of yarn against your face to judge what best suits you.

Seasonal mixtures

The colors of nature—inspired by such things as sunsets, earth tones, and leaves— are more subtle, and a popular choice for men's knits. Combine them in multicolored projects that feature Fair Isle or stripes.

Knitting Abbreviations

This chart includes all the most commonly used abbreviations from knitting instructions. Some patterns may also include some other, special abbreviations, but they are usually explained in the pattern instructions.

alt	alternate	rep	repeat(ing)
beg	begin(ning)	rev st st	reverse stockinette stitch
cm	centimeter(s)	RH	right hand
cont	continu(e)(ing)	RS	right side (of work)
dec	decreas(e)(ing)	s1 k1 psso (skp)	slip one, knit one, pass slipped st over (see p.82)
foll	follow(s)(ing)		
g	gram(s)	s1 k2tog psso (or sk2p)	slip one st, knit 2sts together, pass slipped sts over (see p.83)
g st	garter stitch		
in	inch(es)		
inc	increase(e)(ing)	ssk	slip, slip, knit (see p.82)
k	knit	s	slip stitch(es)
k1 tbl	knit st through back of loop	s2 k1 p2sso	slip 2, knit one, pass slipped stitches over (see p.83)
k2tog (or inc 1)	knit next 2 sts together (see p.80)		
		st(s)	stitch(es)
kfb	knit into front and back of next st (see p.72)	st st	stockinette stitch
		tbl	through back of loop(s)
LH	left hand	tog	together
m	meter(s)	WS	wrong side (of work)
		yd	yard(s)
M1 (or M1k)	make one stitch (see pp.74–75)	yo	yarn forward (US ywfd; see p.76)
mm	millimeter(s)	yo	yarn forward round needle (UK yrfn; see p.78)
oz	ounce(s)		
p	purl	yo	yarn over needle (UK yon; see p.78)
p2tog	purl next 2sts together (see p.81)	yo	yarn round needle (UK yrn; see p.77)
patt	pattern, or work in pattern		
pfb (or inc 1)	purl into front and back of next st (see p.73)	[ ] *	Repeat instructions between brackets, or after or between asterisks, as many times as instructed
psso	pass slipped stitch over		
rem	remain(s)(ing)		

Stitch-symbol Charts

STITCH-SYMBOL CHART

Stitch symbols may also be used to give knitting instructions for stitch patterns in chart form. Some people prefer using stitch-symbol charts, because they find them easier to read. The chart enables them to build up and quickly memorize a visual image of the stitch repeat.

Even with instructions in the form of stitch-symbol charts, written directions for how many stitches to cast on are usually included. If not, it is possible to calculate the cast-on number from the chart, because the number of stitches in the pattern "repeat" will be clearly marked. Cast on a multiple of this number, as well as any edge stitches outside the repeat.

In the chart, each square represents a stitch and each horizontal line of squares stands for a row. Once you have cast on, work upward from the bottom of the chart. Read the odd-numbered rows (usually RS rows) from right to left and the even-numbered rows (usually WS rows) from left to right. Work the edge stitches, then the stitches inside the

repeat, as many times as needed. Some symbols may mean one thing on a RS row and mean another on a WS row (see below).

After you have worked all the charted rows, go back to the bottom of the chart to commence the "row repeat" again.

STITCH SYMBOLS

Symbols in knitting patterns can vary, but here are some of the commonly used knitting symbols that appear in this book. Always follow the explanations given with any pattern—any unusual symbols will be explained in it.

☐ *= k on RS rows, p on WS rows*
◉ *= p on RS rows, k on WS rows*
◙ *= yo (see p.76)*
◿ *= k2tog (see p.80)*
◺ *= ssk (see p.82)*
▲ *= s2 k1 p2sso (see p.83)*

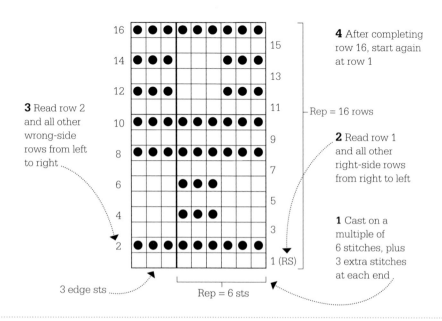

3 Read row 2 and all other wrong-side rows from left to right

4 After completing row 16, start again at row 1

Rep = 16 rows

2 Read row 1 and all other right-side rows from right to left

1 Cast on a multiple of 6 stitches, plus 3 extra stitches at each end

3 edge sts

Rep = 6 sts

1

Start Simple

Learning to knit can be a simple process: it is just a matter of mastering a couple of basic stitches—knit and purl—and understanding a few basic principles, such as getting your gauge right and following a pattern. Once you understand the theory, you can pick up a pair of needles and start clicking. In this chapter, you will discover how to combine those humble knit and purl stitches to stunning effect. Put your newly acquired skills to the test by making a few practical items, including a stylish scarf and cozy patchwork cushion.

Learn to knit:

Simple Bag
pp.46–49

Striped Scarf
pp.56–59

Four-patch Cushion
pp.60–63

How to **Make a Slip Knot**

The initial step in any piece of knitting is to make the very first stitch on one needle. This is formed from a loop of yarn, which is made into what is known as a slip knot. No matter which cast-on method you choose to start with, or what type of fabric you are going to be knitting, the slip knot always comes first.

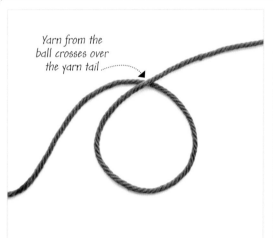

Yarn from the ball crosses over the yarn tail

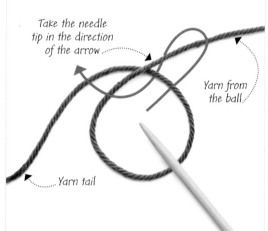

Take the needle tip in the direction of the arrow

Yarn from the ball

Yarn tail

1 Begin by making a loop. To do this, cross the yarn coming from the ball over the end of the yarn. (The yarn end is usually referred to as the yarn "tail.")

2 Take a needle in your right hand. Insert the tip into the loop and out at the top to hook up the yarn leading from the ball. Draw the needle and yarn back through the loop.

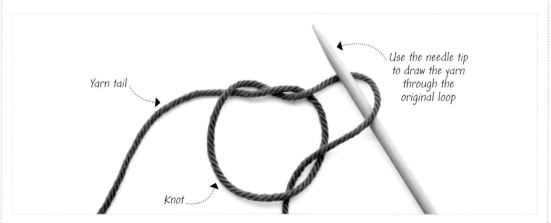

Yarn tail

Use the needle tip to draw the yarn through the original loop

Knot

3 Draw the yarn that has been drawn through the loop toward you at the front and then to the right. You will see the original loop now takes the form of a very loose, open knot below the new loop of yarn on the shaft of the needle.

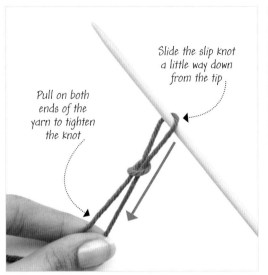

Slide the slip knot a little way down from the tip

Pull on both ends of the yarn to tighten the knot

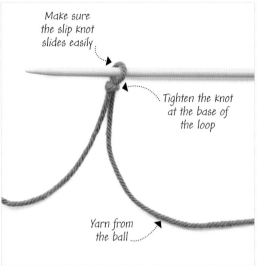

Make sure the slip knot slides easily

Tighten the knot at the base of the loop

Yarn from the ball

4 Tighten the knot by pulling on both the yarn ends with your left hand. Position the loop of the slip knot on the shaft—not the tapered tip—of the needle.

5 When you tighten the knot, do not tighten it too much. Make sure that you can still slide the loop of the knot easily along the shaft of the needle.

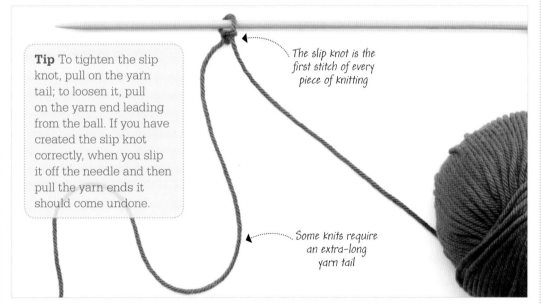

Tip To tighten the slip knot, pull on the yarn tail; to loosen it, pull on the yarn end leading from the ball. If you have created the slip knot correctly, when you slip it off the needle and then pull the yarn ends it should come undone.

The slip knot is the first stitch of every piece of knitting

Some knits require an extra-long yarn tail

6 Practice this method of forming a slip knot until you master it. As a general rule, the yarn tail should be about 6–8 in (15–20 cm)

long; it will be darned in later or used to stitch a seam. Some knitting patterns, however, may require you to leave an extra-long yarn tail.

How to **Hold Yarn and Needles**

Here are two different methods of holding yarn and needles: "English" and "Continental." Knitting is ambidextrous, so one of these commonly used styles should suit you, whether you are right-handed or left-handed. Try both ways to discover which works best and feels most comfortable and natural for you.

English style

Weave the yarn through your fingers ....

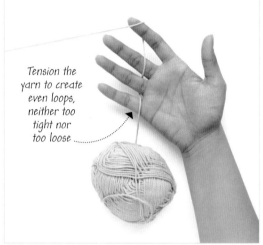

Tension the yarn to create even loops, neither too tight nor too loose ....

1 Lace the yarn around the fingers of your right hand. Keep your hand relaxed, so the yarn is not pulled too tightly and can flow through your fingers as you knit.

2 Alternatively, try other ways of looping the yarn in and out of your fingers, but in a way that allows you to control the yarn as it passes through your fingers to form stitches.

The left needle holds stitches to be worked ....

...The right hand controls the yarn coming from the ball

3 As you knit, you will need to hold in your left hand the needle that is loaded with the stitches about to be worked. Hold the other needle in your right hand, using your right forefinger to guide the yarn around the needle.

Continental style

Choose a way to loop the yarn that feels comfortable

Here, the yarn is wrapped twice around the left forefinger

1 Lace the yarn in uniform loops through the fingers of your left hand. Keep your hand relaxed so that the yarn can flow through your your fingers easily.

2 Experiment with different ways of lacing the yarn through your fingers until you find one that allows you to tension and release the yarn comfortably in uniform loops.

Use your left forefinger to guide the yarn

The right hand controls the needle forming a new stitch

3 As you knit, you will need to hold the needle with the stitches to be worked in your left hand and the other needle in your right hand. Manipulate the yarn with your left forefinger, pulling it through the stitch loops with the tip of the right needle.

How to **Knit Knit On Cast On**

Casting on creates a foundation row of stitches, forming the basis of your knit fabric. The simple cast-on method shown here uses just one strand and is also known as the "knit-stretch cast on." Knit on cast on uses two needles to create a succession of new stitches from the initial slip knot.

Tip Beginners usually knit too tightly, making it difficult to slide the stitches along the needle. To avoid this, make sure you form each stitch on the shaft of the needle and not on the tip.

Yarn from ball

Long tail of yarn

1 Hold the yarn in your left or right hand (see pp.32–33). Take the needle with the slip knot in your left hand and insert the tip of the right needle—approaching from right to left—through the loop of the slip knot, so it is behind the left needle.

The slip knot should be loose enough to accommodate both needles

Insert the right needle into the slip knot, behind the left needle

2 Take the yarn behind both of your needles and wrap it under and around the tip of the right needle. Be careful not to pull the yarn too tightly as you do this, otherwise you will tighten the slip knot.

This loop forms a new stitch

3 Use the tip of the right needle to draw the yarn up through the slip knot. The name of this cast-on method comes from the fact that this is also the way to form a knit stitch.

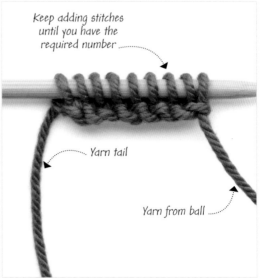

Catch the loop to form a new stitch

Yarn from ball

Yarn tail

4 Use the right needle to draw the loop to the right and over the tip of the left needle, where it will form a new stitch.

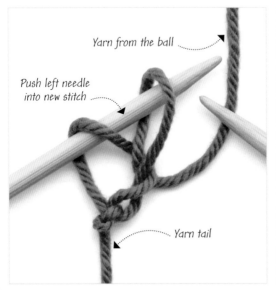

Yarn from the ball

Push left needle into new stitch

Yarn tail

5 Pull both yarn ends to tighten the newly formed—or cast-on—loop and slide this new stitch up close to the slip knot.

Keep adding stitches until you have the required number

Yarn tail

Yarn from ball

6 Continue in the same way, casting on new stitches, until you have the number required by your pattern.

How to **Knit Cable Cast On**

This straight-forward, single-strand cast-on method creates a firm, ropelike edge that is not very stretchy. It is particularly useful for casting on extra stitches at the edge of the work within a pattern. The first stitch of the cable cast on (not including the slip knot) is formed in the same way as the knit-on cast-on method (see pp.34–35).

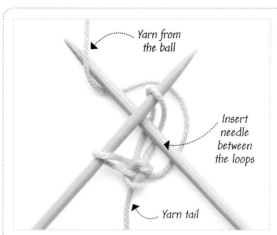

Yarn from the ball

Insert needle between the loops

Yarn tail

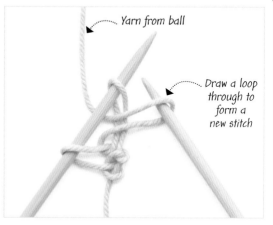

Yarn from ball

Draw a loop through to form a new stitch

1 Create two stitches on the left needle as for the knit on cast on (see pp.34–35). Push the right needle tip between the two loops, then wrap the yarn under and around it.

2 Draw the yarn back through the two loops with the right needle tip, to form a new stitch on the tip of the right needle.

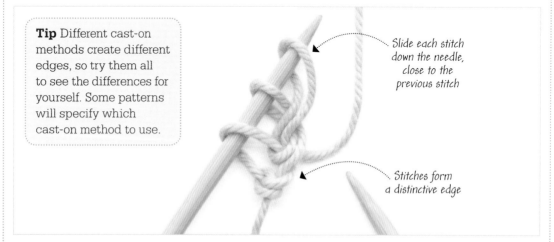

Tip Different cast-on methods create different edges, so try them all to see the differences for yourself. Some patterns will specify which cast-on method to use.

Slide each stitch down the needle, close to the previous stitch

Stitches form a distinctive edge

3 Transfer the loop on the right-hand needle to the left-hand needle. Continue, inserting the right-hand needle between the first two loops on the left needle when beginning each new cast-on stitch.

How to **Knit Backward Loop Cast On**

This method, which is also known as the "thumb" cast on, uses only one needle and creates a soft edge that can be put to use in most situations. It is probably the simplest to learn and is quick to do. You start off by creating a slip knot (see pp.30–31) on one needle and then you hold the needle in your right hand.

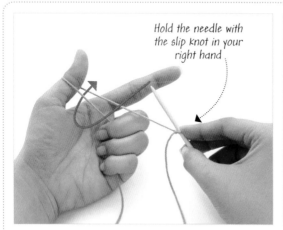

Hold the needle with the slip knot in your right hand

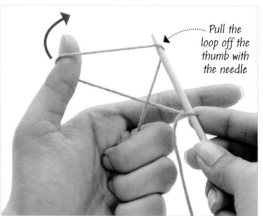

Pull the loop off the thumb with the needle

1 Wrap the yarn from the ball around your left thumb, securing the strand under your fingers. Insert the needle tip up through the loop on your thumb, as shown by the arrow.

2 Release the loop from your thumb, and pull the yarn from the ball to tighten the loop and create a new stitch. Slide the new stitch along the needle, close to the slip knot.

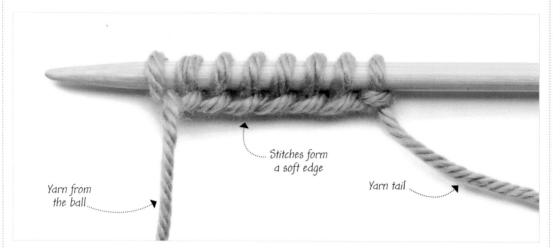

Stitches form a soft edge

Yarn from the ball

Yarn tail

3 Create the number of stitches that the pattern requires, by continuing to loop the yarn from the ball around your left thumb, picking up each loop in turn with the needle in the right hand, and sliding it along, close to the previous stitch.

How to **Long-tail Cast On**

This cast-on method, also called the knit double cast on, creates a versatile edge that is both strong and stretchy. Two strands—one from the tail and one from the ball—are used to create the cast-on stitches. When creating the initial slip knot, you will need to leave a yarn tail at least three times as long as the width of your planned knit piece.

Long yarn tail

Yarn from the ball

Secure both strands under the fingers of your left hand

> **Tip** Another method of figuring out how long the yarn tail should be is to allow approximately 1½in (3.5 cm) for each stitch you will be casting on.

Pull out the loop with the needle tip

1 Hold the needle with the slip knot in your right hand. Loop the long yarn tail over your left thumb and the ball yarn over your left forefinger. Lock both strands in your left palm.

2 Insert the tip of the needle under the strand of yarn held between your left thumb and fingers. Take the needle upward and outward to create a loop.

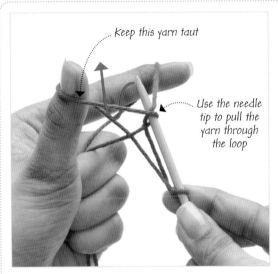

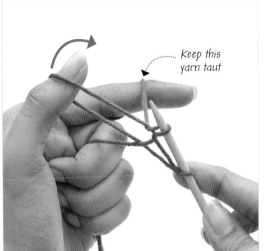

3 Insert the needle, from right to left, behind the strand that is between your forefinger and palm. Pull that strand through the loop on your thumb, as shown by the arrow.

4 You should now have a loop on the needle. Release the loop of yarn from around your thumb, while keeping both strands held in your left palm quite taut.

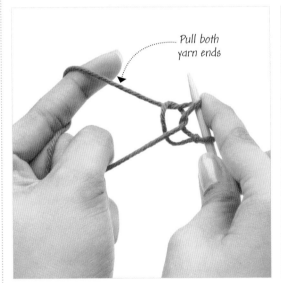

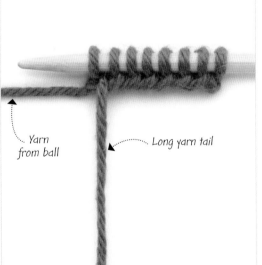

5 To tighten the loop on the needle and create the new stitch, pull both yarn ends. At the same time, slide the new stitch with your right forefinger down the needle, until it is close to the slip knot.

6 Loop the yarn from the long tail over your thumb again and cast on another stitch, as described in steps 1 to 5. Repeat the process until you have the required number of stitches on your needle.

How to **Knit Knit Stitch** (Abbreviation = k)

Once you have cast on the number of stitches you need, it is time to start creating a knit fabric. Rows of knit stitch form a fabric known as "garter stitch," which looks the same on both sides (see p.124), but the fabric shown on these pages is "stockinette stitch," which is formed of alternate rows of knit and purl stitches.

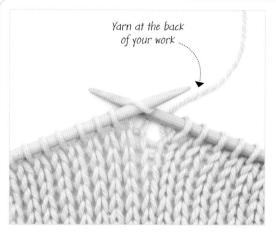

Yarn at the back of your work

1 Hold the needle with unworked stitches in your left hand. With the yarn at the back, insert the tip of the right needle into the next stitch, from front to back, on the left needle.

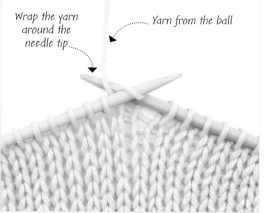

Wrap the yarn around the needle tip

Yarn from the ball

2 Take the yarn from behind both needles, and wrap it under and around the tip of the right needle. Hold the yarn firmly but not too tightly.

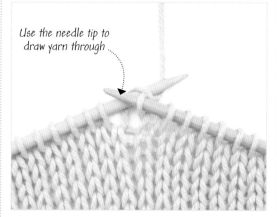

Use the needle tip to draw yarn through

3 Pull the tip of the right needle toward you, drawing the loop of yarn through the stitch on the left needle and keeping an even tension as the yarn slips through your fingers.

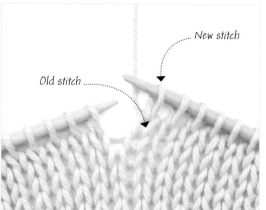

New stitch

Old stitch

4 Let the old stitch slip off the left needle as the new loop creates a fresh stitch on the right needle. Work all the stitches from the left needle in this way to the end of the row.

How to **Knit Purl Stitch** (Abbreviation = p)

Knit fabric is made from two basic stitches: knit and purl. The purl stitch is the bumpy back of the knit stitch. It takes a little more practice than knit stitch to master, but is still relatively easy. You may find your tension alters on purl stitches, in which case you will need to hold your yarn slightly tighter or looser to compensate.

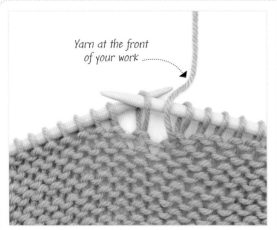

Yarn at the front of your work

Wrap the yarn around the needle tip *Yarn from the ball*

1 Hold the needle with unworked stitches in your left hand. Holding the yarn in front, insert the right needle tip from right to left into the next stitch on the left needle.

2 Take the yarn from the front of the work back toward the right needle and wrap it over and around the tip. Hold the yarn firmly but not too tightly.

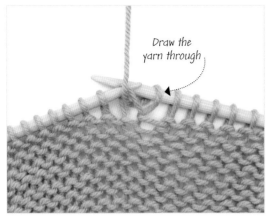

Draw the yarn through

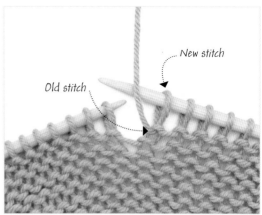

Old stitch *New stitch*

3 Pull the tip of the right needle away from you, drawing the loop of yarn through the stitch on the left needle, and keeping an even tension as the yarn slips through your fingers.

4 Let the old stitch slip off the left needle as the new loop creates a fresh stitch on the right needle. Work all the stitches from the left needle in this way to the end of the row.

How to **Knit Cast Offs**

When you have completed work on a piece of knit fabric, you usually need to close off the loops so that they will not unravel when you remove them from the needles. This process is called "casting off." Casting off knitwise and casting off purlwise are the most basic and easiest of casting off techniques.

Casting off knitwise

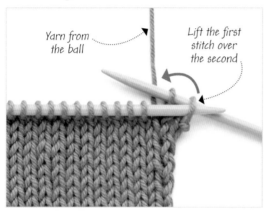

Yarn from the ball

Lift the first stitch over the second

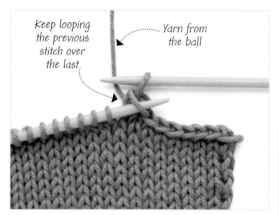

Keep looping the previous stitch over the last

Yarn from the ball

1 Knit the first two stitches of the row. Insert the left needle tip from left to right into the first of these stitches; then lift it up and over the second stitch, and off the needle.

2 Knit another stitch from the left needle so you have two stitches on the right needle again. Lift the first stitch up and over the second stitch. Repeat to the end of the row.

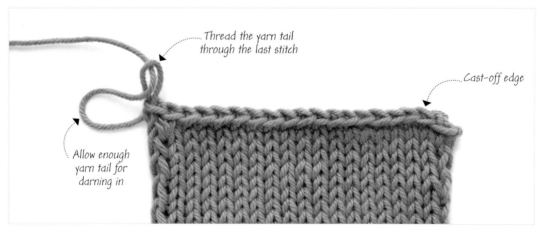

Thread the yarn tail through the last stitch

Cast-off edge

Allow enough yarn tail for darning in

3 When there is only one stitch remaining, cut the yarn, leaving a yarn tail about 8 in (20 cm) long (so that it can be darned in later).

Pass the yarn tail through the loop of the remaining stitch, then pull the tail tight to close the loop and fasten off the knitting.

Casting off purlwise

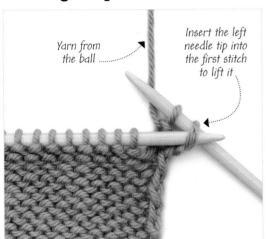

Yarn from the ball ......▸

Insert the left needle tip into the first stitch to lift it

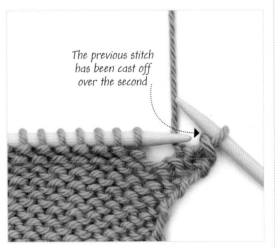

The previous stitch has been cast off over the second

1 Purl two stitches (see p.41), then take the yarn to the back of the work. Use the tip of the left needle to lift the first stitch over the second stitch and off the needle.

2 Bring the yarn to the front and purl another stitch. Then repeat the process of passing the first of the two stitches on the right needle over the second stitch and off.

Slipping stitches off the needle

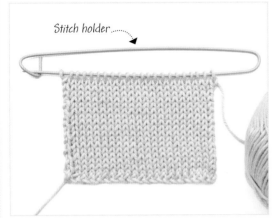

Stitch holder ......▸

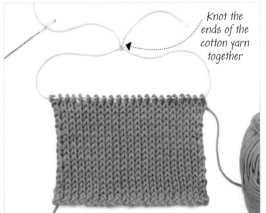

Knot the ends of the cotton yarn together

USING A STITCH HOLDER

If you are setting stitches aside to work on later, instead of casting off, simply slide the stitches carefully from your needle to a stitch holder. If you have only a few stitches, you could use a safety pin or paper clip.

USING A LENGTH OF YARN

If you don't have a stitch holder, slip the stitches onto a length of cotton yarn. Thread the cotton yarn into a blunt-ended yarn needle and thread through the stitch loops before slipping them off your knitting needle.

How to **Knit Seams**

The examples on these pages show yarns of a contrasting color used to join pieces of knit fabric together, but you should use the same yarn as you used for knitting. In most cases, seams need to be as neat and invisible as possible; messy seams spoil the look of a finished item. Pattern instructions usually offer guidance about which method to use.

Mattress stitch

1 This method is used to join two side edges of knitting and is the best choice for stockinette stitch and ribbed fabrics. Align the two edges to be joined, right sides facing upward, and secure the yarn at the base of one of the edges.

2 Insert the needle from the front through the center of the first knit stitch on one side and up through the center of the stitch two rows above. Repeat on the other side and continue, from side to side, up the seam, then pull the yarn to close the two sides together.

Edge-to-edge

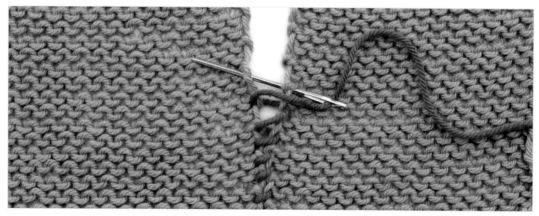

Use this method for any knit fabric; garter stitch fabric is used here. Align the edges of the two pieces with wrong sides facing you.

Anchor the yarn at the base of one edge and take the needle through the little "bumps" of yarn along the edges, as shown.

Grafted seam

Stitch across both edges to create one seam

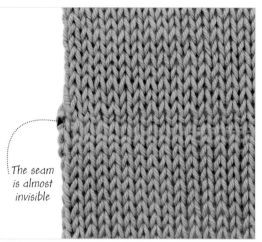

The seam is almost invisible

1 Use this method to join two cast-off edges. Align the pieces, right sides up. Insert the needle under each knit stitch along both seams, zigzagging from one side to the other.

2 Pull the yarn gently, until the two edges are closed together to create a virtually invisible seam. Darn in the end of the yarn to secure it.

Backstitch seam

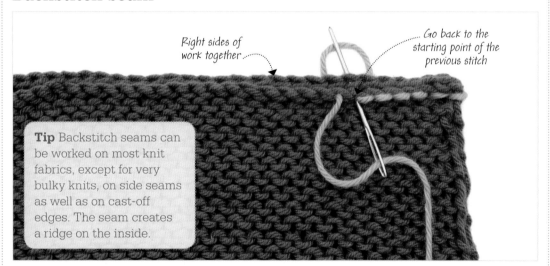

Right sides of work together

Go back to the starting point of the previous stitch

Tip Backstitch seams can be worked on most knit fabrics, except for very bulky knits, on side seams as well as on cast-off edges. The seam creates a ridge on the inside.

Align the edges of the pieces to be joined, with right sides together. Secure the yarn on the right-hand edge, then make one stitch forward. Bring the needle back to the starting point of the previous stitch, and repeat. Stitch as close to the edges of the fabric pieces as possible, so that the finished inside seam is not too bulky.

Knit a Simple Knit Bag

An ideal first project, the main part of this bag is made from a rectangle of garter-stitch fabric. The strap—just a mere strip of knitting—is also in garter stitch, with buttons stitched at the joining points.

Instructions

Difficulty Level
Easy

Size
4½ x 3½ in (12 x 8.5 cm)

Yarn
Berroco Vintage DK 100 g
A: 21190 Cerulean x 1
B: 398 Fondant x 1

Needles
1 pair of US6 (4 mm/UK8) needles
Blunt tapestry needle

Notions
Two 15 mm buttons

Gauge
21 sts and 42 rows to 4 in (10 cm)
over g st using US6 (4 mm/UK8)
needles

21190
Cerulean x 1

398
Fondant x 1

1 pair of US6 (4mm/UK8) needles

1 Use US6 (4mm/UK8) needles and yarn A to cast on 20 stitches, using the knit-on cast-on method (see pp.34–35). Then work in garter stitch—which means you knit every row.

Remember If you knit looser than the one noted on p.47, your bag will end up bigger than the one shown. If you knit tighter, your bag will be smaller when it is finished.

Knit the main part in garter stitch

Cast off the stitches one by one

Stitches yet to be cast off

2 When your piece of knitting measures 10 in (24 cm) from the cast-on edge to the top of the row still on the needle, it is time to cast off. For full instructions on how to do this, see "Casting off knitwise," p.42. When you cut the yarn, be sure to leave a tail about 12 in (30 cm) long, for sewing up.

Careful! Try to cast off loosely; if you pull each stitch too tight, the edge of the work will be too small.

3 To make your strip of knitting into a bag, fold it in half so that the cast-on and cast-off edges are together and the wrong sides of the knitting are on the outside. Thread the tail of yarn into a blunt-ended tapestry needle and sew both side seams. You can whip stitch them, or work in backstitch (see p.45). Until you are more experienced with making up, choose whichever method you feel most comfortable with. Then turn your bag the right way out.

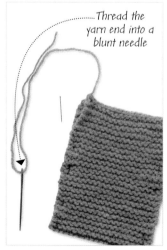

Thread the yarn end into a blunt needle

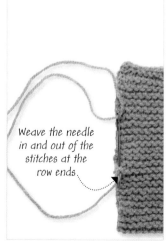

Weave the needle in and out of the stitches at the row ends

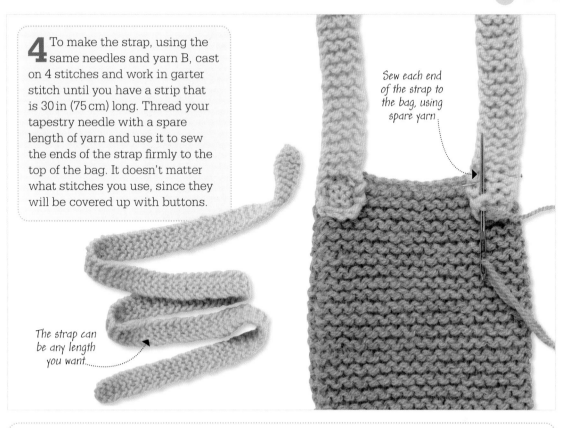

4 To make the strap, using the same needles and yarn B, cast on 4 stitches and work in garter stitch until you have a strip that is 30 in (75 cm) long. Thread your tapestry needle with a spare length of yarn and use it to sew the ends of the strap firmly to the top of the bag. It doesn't matter what stitches you use, since they will be covered up with buttons.

Sew each end of the strap to the bag, using spare yarn

The strap can be any length you want

The perfect **Knit Bag**

A small purse like this one is a good project for a beginner to tackle, because it is easy and quick to make. It also tests your skills in simple finishing techniques.

Straight edges
If the side edges of your knitting are wavy, there is a simple way to remedy this. Instead of knitting the first stitch in every row, try slipping it from the left needle, straight onto the right needle, then knit the second stitch and every other stitch to the end of the row.

Secure seaming
Make sure you sew sturdy seams and that the ends of the strap are sewn securely to the bag. You

shouldn't worry if your stitches don't look perfect, since they will be covered by the buttons. You can always improve the neatness of your stitches as you progress to more complex knitting projects.

Smooth fabric
Don't worry at this stage if your knitting looks a bit uneven: garter stitch is a ridged fabric that is not particularly smooth. It was chosen for this project because it is easy, but you will soon progress to more attractive, sophisticated fabrics.

Also learn to make ▶ ▶ ▶

Knit a Phone Case

A cute case for your mobile phone, like the Simple Knit Bag (see pp.46–49), can be made from a knit rectangle folded in half. The main fabric is in stockinette stitch, with a couple of ridges for decorative interest.

Instructions

Difficulty Level
Easy

Size
4½ x 2⅜in (11.5 x 6 cm)

Yarn
Rowan Pure Wool DK 50 g

A: 19 Avocado x 1

Sirdar Country Style DK 50 g

B: 398 Macaroon x 1

Needles
1 pair of US6 (4 mm/UK8) needles

Gauge
22 sts and 28 rows to 4 in (10 cm) over sts st on US6 (4 mm/UK8) needles

Special Abbreviations
S1p Slip one stitch purlwise

Pattern

Using US6 (4 mm/UK8) needles and yarn A, cast on 18 sts.
Row 1: K.
Row 2: P.
Rep rows 1 and 2 (stockinette stitch) 6 times.
Row 15: P.
Row 16: K.
Rep rows 1–16 four times more, then rows 1 and 2 six times more, until work measures 9 in (23 cm), ending with RS facing.
Cast off loosely and fasten off, leaving a long tail of yarn.

Button loop
Using US6 (4 mm/UK8) needles and yarn B, cast on 24 stitches, turn, and cast off.

Finishing
Fold knit fabric in half with wrong sides together and ends matching. Sew side seams in backstitch (see p.45). Weave in all yarn ends. Turn right side out. For the button loop, form the strip of knitting into a loop and stitch the ends together. Sew the loop to the top of the back section of the cover. Sew a button to the front of the cover, close to the top edge.

Knit a Tablet Cover

By using a particular type of variegated yarn (one that is dyed in sections, with regular color changes along the strand of yarn), you can create a mock Fair Isle effect. Knit in stocking stitch, this clever cover-up is made in a similar way to the Simple Knit Bag (see pp.46–49).

Instructions

Difficulty Level
Easy

Size
9$\frac{1}{2}$ x 7$\frac{1}{2}$ in (24 cm x 19 cm)

Yarn
Sirdar Crofter Fair Isle Effect DK 50 g
059 Rambler Rose x 1

Needles
1 pair of US6 (4 mm/UK8) needles

Gauge
22 sts and 28 rows to 4 in (10 cm) over st st on US6 (4 mm/UK8) needles

Pattern
Using US6 (4 mm/UK8) needles, cast on 40 sts.
Row 1: K.
Row 2: P
Rep rows 1 and 2 (stockinette stitch) until work measures 19$\frac{1}{2}$ in (49 cm), ending with RS facing. Cast off loosely and fasten off, leaving a long tail of yarn.

Making up
Fold the knit fabric in half, with WS together and ends matching, and sew side seams in backstitch (see p.45). Weave in all yarn ends.Block, using the wet blocking method (see p.141).

How to **Add a New Color**

Even experienced knitters don't always know the best way to join in a new ball of yarn. When you are nearing the end of a ball, to calculate if you have enough yarn for two more rows, fold the remaining yarn in half and make a slip knot at the fold. Knit one row and if you reach the knot before the end of the row, it's time to start a new ball.

Tie the new yarn to the old yarn with a loose knot

Knit using the new yarn

1 Always try to join in a new ball—whether it is a different color or the same one—at the beginning of a row. Knot the end of the new yarn loosely onto the old yarn.

2 Slide the knot up close to the edge of the knitting and continue knitting, using the new yarn. Don't worry about the loose ends at this stage: they can be dealt with later.

Thread the yarn onto a needle

Weave in yarn ends as you knit

3 To darn loose ends, thread the yarn onto a blunt-ended needle and weave it in and out of the stitches along the edge of the knitting, then trim off the remaining end.

4 Another way of dealing with ends when joining in a new ball is to weave one or both of the yarn ends across the wrong side of the work as you knit with the new yarn.

How to **Darn Ends**

Many patterns instruct you, when you come to the end of a section, to fasten off your knitting and leave a tail of yarn: this is usually required for the sewing-up process. You are also likely to have additional ends to deal with. Here are some basic tips for keeping your knitting neat, tidy, and free from stray yarn ends.

Open up the last stitch

1 When you come to the end of a cast-off row, you will be left with one stitch on the right needle. Pull the needle upward to open up the stitch loop slightly.

Hold the base of the loop in your left hand

Place the yarn end into the loop

2 Cut the yarn, leaving a short tail (unless instructed to leave a long tail), and insert the end of this tail through the center of the stitch loop.

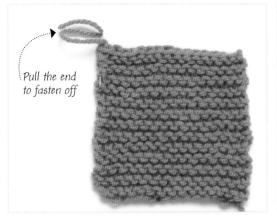

Pull the end to fasten off

3 Pull the yarn tail to close up the loop; this is called "fastening off." You will now be left with a tail of yarn that needs to be woven in neatly.

Weave in the yarn end down the side

4 Thread the yarn end into a blunt-ended needle and weave the needle in and out of the stitches at the side of the work for about 2 in (5 cm), then trim off the remaining yarn.

How to **Make a Fringe**

Fringe is easy to add to a knit piece, for a traditional, decorative edge finish. It could be in a color that matches or contrasts with the main knit fabric and can be added to the ends or selvedges of the piece when the knitting has been completed. When planning your project, remember to allow extra yarn for the fringe.

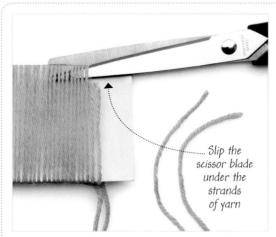

... Slip the scissor blade under the strands of yarn

... Pull the loop to the back, then pull the strands through the loop

1 Cut a rectangle of cardboard slightly wider than the desired fringe length. Wind yarn around it; cut through the loops on one side to produce strands twice the width of the card.

2 Take several strands, folded in half; hold the loops in front of the fabric edge. Insert a crochet hook through the back of the fabric, close to the seam, and pull the loops through.

... Fringes could be in the same or a contrasting color or yarn

3 With the loop still on the hook, catch the strands in the crochet hook and pull them through the loop until securely knotted.

Repeat the process to add more fringe at intervals along the edge, then trim all the ends to the same length.

How to **Make Tassels**

Making a tassel is a good way of using up leftover yarn and it can be used to embellish various items such as the top of a hat or the ends of a scarf or light sweater, or the corners of a cushion cover or a knit throw. You could also use them to decorate other, non-knit handmade items, such as lamp shades or bags.

Knot a double strand of yarn tightly, leaving long ends

1 Cut a cardboard rectangle slightly wider than the desired tassel length. Wind about 50 loops of yarn around the card. Thread a double strand of yarn through them to secure.

Cut through the yarn loops

2 Insert the blades of your scissors through the loops at the base of the tassel, cut through all the strands, and remove the cardboard template.

Sew the yarn ends through the tassel head

3 Bind a length of yarn around the top, a little below the knot of double yarn, to create a "head." Tie securely and sew the yarn ends through the tassel head a few times.

Trim the yarn ends to create an even edge

4 Leave one long length of yarn emerging from the top of the tassel and use this to sew or tie the tassel in place. Trim the ends of the tassel to an even length.

Knit a Striped Scarf

This vibrant scarf is an enjoyable, simple way to build your knitting rhythm and skills. Knit in a single rib (see p.64), which forms a double-sided fabric, it involves frequent color changes. Add a fringe in your choice of remaining yarn.

Instructions

Difficulty Level
Easy

Size
71 in (180 cm) or desired length

Yarn
Rowan Pure Wool DK 50 g
A: 028 Raspberry x 2 B: 026
Hyacinth x 3 C: 047 Geranium x 1
D: 042 Dahlia x 2 E: 030 Damson x 1

Needles
A: 1 pair of US6 (4 mm/UK8) needles

Gauge
22 sts and 30 rows to 4 in (10 cm)
over st st on US6 (4 mm/UK8)
needles

Special Abbreviations
S1p Slip one stitch purlwise

Pattern
Using US6 (4 mm/UK8) needles
and yarn A, cast on 50 sts.
Row 1 (RS): S1p, p1, [k1, p1] to end.
Row 2: S1p, p1, [k1, p1] to end.
These 2 rows form a 1 x 1 rib with
a slipped stitch at the beginning
of each row.
Repeat these 2 rows six times
more (14 rows worked in total),
ending with a WS row.
Join in yarn B using a slip knot
(see p.30).
Work in 14-row stripes of rib in the
following color sequence: C, B, A,
D, E, D, A, B. Repeat four times.
To finish stripe sequence, work
14-row stripes in color C, B, then
A. Cast off in rib.
Cut yarn B (or your choice of yarn)
into lengths approximately 9 in
(22 cm) long. Affix these as a fringe
along each end of the scarf using
the method shown on p.54.

**028
Raspberry x 2**

**026
Hyacinth x 3**

**047
Geranium x 1**

**042
Dahlia x 2**

**1 pair of US6
(4 mm/UK8) needles**

**030
Damson x 1**

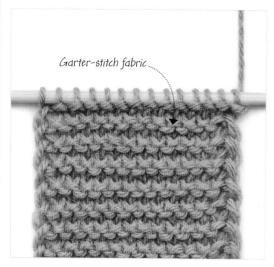

Garter-stitch fabric

Stockinette-stitch fabric

Selvedges

Where the sides of a piece of knitting (the selvedges) can be seen, rather than being hidden within a seam, they should be as neat as possible. This pattern employs a chain selvedge, which looks equally neat on garter-stitch and stockinette-stitch fabrics.

A generous fringe is the perfect finishing touch

Fringe

Leave a small gap between each set of fringe, because if the knots are too close together, they will stretch and distort the edge.

You could substitute spare yarn in any color when making the fringe

Ribbing (formed by knitting and purling alternate stitches) creates a double-sided fabric

For tips on changing colors, see p.52

Weave in all yarn ends along the sides of the scarf

A few purple stripes among the shades of red create visual interest

Color changes

On a double-sided fabric such as this single rib, color changes remain neat on both sides of the fabric. You will have a lot of yarn ends to deal with: weave them in neatly along the sides of the scarf, to prevent unsightly ridges.

Knit a Four-patch Cushion

Knit in a super-chunky yarn for speedy results, this cushion is an ideal project for beginners because it requires no shaping. You just need to know how to knit in garter stitch, add in a new color, and how to sew pieces together.

Instructions

Difficulty level
Easy

Size
20 x 20 in (50 x 50 cm)

Yarn
Blue Sky Alpaca Bulky
A: colorway 1212 Grasshopper x 3
B: 1222 Seaweed x 2
C: 1000 Angora x 2

Needles
1 pair of US17 (12 mm) needles

Notions
20 in (50 cm) zipper (optional)
20 x 20 in (50 x 50 cm) cushion pad
  or polyester stuffing

Gauge
8 sts and 12 rows to 4 in (10 cm) over g st

**1222
Seaweed x 2**

**1212
Grasshopper x 3**

**1000
Angora x 2**

1 pair of US17 (12 mm) needles

Pattern

The cushion cover is constructed of four strips, worked bottom to top, as follows:

Strip 1 (make 2)

Using yarn A, and US17 (12 mm) needles, cast on 21 sts. Work 30 rows in g st (k every row).
Change to yarn B, and work 30 rows. Cast off.

Strip 2 (make 2)

Using yarn C, and US17 (12 mm) needles, cast on 21 sts. Work 30 rows in g st. Change to yarn A, and work 30 rows. Cast off.

Finishing

Lay strips alongside each other, in order, using the photograph (see opposite) as a guide, to form the two sides. Sew up each side, with WS facing, using an edge-to-edge seam (see p.44). Whip stitch three sides of the cushion, with WS facing, and add polyester stuffing, or insert a cushion pad, then sew remaining side closed. Darn in all yarn ends. Cut 12 strands of spare yarn, each 6 in (15 cm) long, and insert three into each corner, as if you were making a fringe (see p.54).

Edge-to-edge seam

Align the edges of the knit pieces, with wrong sides up, and stitch together, inserting the needle through the little bumps on the selvedges (see also p.44). You can create a similar seam by placing the two pieces of knitting, right sides together, and whip stitching the edges.

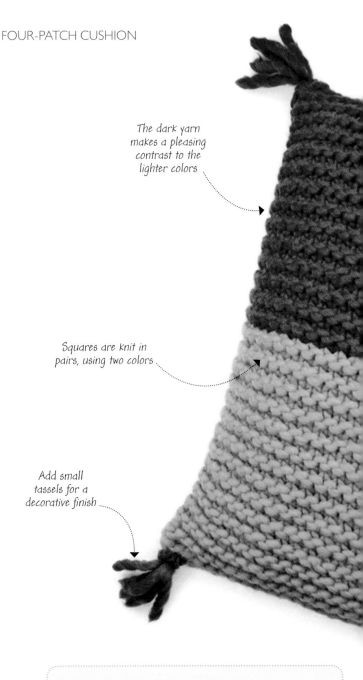

The dark yarn makes a pleasing contrast to the lighter colors

Squares are knit in pairs, using two colors

Add small tassels for a decorative finish

Tassels

To create these simple tassels, insert several strands of yarn into each corner, pull them through, and knot, in a similar way to making a fringe (see p.54).

Remember There are various ways of sewing seams to join pieces of knitting together. For this project, an edge-to-edge seam, or a whip-stitch seam, is appropriate because it blends well into the ridged texture of the garter-stitch fabric.

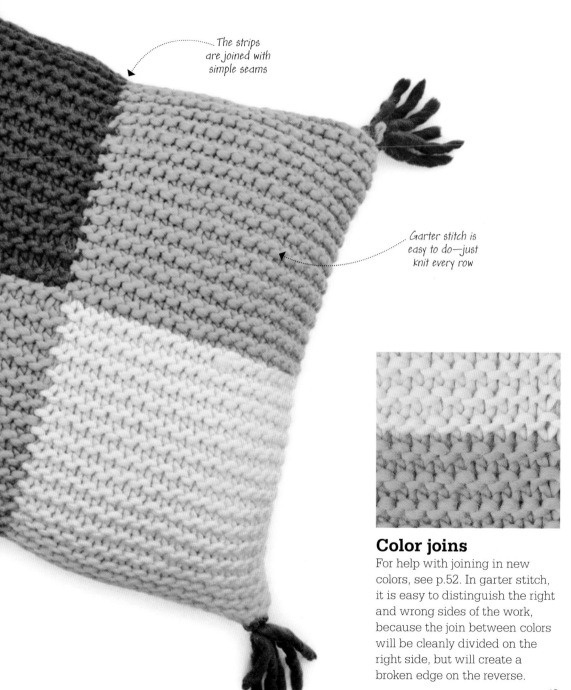

...The strips are joined with simple seams

Garter stitch is easy to do—just knit every row

Color joins

For help with joining in new colors, see p.52. In garter stitch, it is easy to distinguish the right and wrong sides of the work, because the join between colors will be cleanly divided on the right side, but will create a broken edge on the reverse.

63

Gallery of **Simple Stitch Patterns**

By combining knit and purl stitches, you can easily create a wealth of different patterns. Unlike stockinette stitch, each one of these patterns produces a flat, reversible knit fabric—and, whereas stockinette stitch has a tendency to curl at the edges, these fabrics do not curl but lie flat, making them suitable for scarves, throws, and blankets.

Single Rib

Instructions

For an even number of sts:
Row 1: *K1, p1, rep from * to end.
Rep row 1 to form patt.

For an odd number of sts:
Row 1: *K1, p1, rep from * to last st, k1.
Row 2: *P1, k1, rep from * to last st, p1.
Rep rows 1 and 2 to form patt.

Double Rib

Instructions

Cast on a multiple of 4sts.
Row 1: *K2, p2, rep from *.
Rep row 1 to form patt.

Traveling Rib

Instructions

Cast on a multiple of 4sts.
Row 1 (RS): *K2, p2, rep from * to end.
Row 2: As row 1.
Row 3: *K1, p2, k1, rep from * to end.
Row 4: *P1, k2, p1, rep from * to end.
Row 5: *P2, k2, rep from * to end.
Row 6: As row 5.
Row 7: As row 4.
Row 8: As row 3.
Rep rows 1–8 to form patt.

Fisherman's Rib

Instructions

Cast on an odd number of sts and knit 1 row.
Row 1 (RS): S1, *k1 tbl, p1, rep from * to end.
Row 2: S1, *p1, k1 tbl, rep from * to last 2sts, p1, k1.
Rep rows 1 and 2 to form patt.

English Rib

Instructions

Cast on an odd number of sts.
Row 1: S1, *p1, k1, rep from * to end.
Row 2: S1, *k1 tbl, p1, rep from * to end.
Rep rows 1 and 2 to form patt.

Broken Rib

Instructions

Cast on a multiple of 4sts plus 2 extra sts.
Row 1 (RS): *K3, p1, rep from * to last 2sts, k2.
Row 2: P1, *k3, p1, rep from * to last st, k1.

Seed Stitch

Instructions

For an even number of sts:
Row 1: *K1, p1, rep from * to end.
Row 2: *P1, k1, rep from * to end.
Rep rows 1 and 2 to form patt.

For an odd number of sts:
Row 1: *K1, p1, rep from * to last st, k1.
Rep row 1 to form patt.

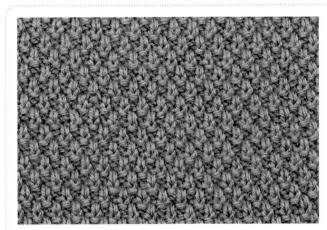

Moss Stitch

Instructions

Cast on an odd number of sts.
Row 1 (RS): *K1, p1, rep from * to last st, k1.
Row 2: *P1, k1, rep from * to last st, p1.
Row 3: As row 2.
Row 4: As row 1.
Rep rows 1–4 to form patt.

Broken Seed Stitch

Instructions

Cast on an odd number of sts.
Row 1 (RS): *P1, k1, rep from * to last st, k1.
Row 2: K.
Rep rows 1 and 2 to form patt.

Stockinette Box Stitch

Instructions

Cast on a multiple of 10sts plus 5 extra sts.
Row 1 (RS): *K5, p5, rep from * to last 5sts, k5.
Row 2: P.
Repeat last 2 rows twice more, then
row 1 again.
Row 8: K5, *p5, k5, rep from * to end.
Row 9: K.
Repeat last 2 rows twice more, then
row 8 again. Rep rows 1–14 to form patt.

Striped Box Stitch
Instructions

Cast on a multiple of 6sts plus 3 extra sts.
Row 1 and all odd-numbered rows (RS): K.
Row 2: K.
Rows 4 and 6: P3, *k3, p3, rep from * to end.
Row 8 and 10: K.
Rows 12 and 14: K3, *p3, k3, rep from * to end.
Row 16: K.
Rep rows 1–16 to form patt.

Textured Check Stitch
Instructions

Cast on a multiple of 4sts plus 3 extra sts.
Row 1: K3, *p1, k3, rep from * to end.
Row 2: K1, *p1, k3, rep from * to last 2sts, p1, k1.
Rows 3–6: [Rep rows 1 and 2] twice.
Row 7: K1, *p1, k3, rep from * to last 2sts, p1, k1.
Row 8: K3, *p1, k3, rep from * to end.
Rows 9–12: [Rep rows 7 and 8] twice.
Rep rows 1–12 to form patt.

Diamond Stitch
Instructions

Cast on a multiple of 9sts.
Row 1 (RS): K2, *p5, k4, rep from * to last 7sts, p5, k2.
Row 2: P1, *k7, p2, rep from * to last 8sts, k7, p1.
Row 3: P.
Row 4: Rep row 2.
Row 5: Rep row 1.
Row 6: P3, *k3, p6, rep from * to last 6sts, k3, p3.
Row 7: K4, *p1, k8, rep from * to last 5sts, p1, k4.
Row 8: Rep row 6.
Rep rows 1–8 to form patt.

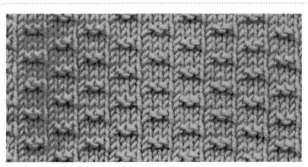

Double Seed Stitch

Instructions

Cast on a multiple of 6sts plus 2 extra sts.
Row 1 (RS): K.
Row 2: K2, *p4, k2, rep from * to end.
Row 3: As row 1.
Row 4: P2, *p1, k2, p3, rep from * to end.
Rep rows 1–4 to form patt.

Basketweave Stitch

Instructions

Cast on a multiple of 8sts.
Rows 1–5: *K4, p4, rep from * to end.
Rows 6–10: *P4, k4, rep from * to end.
Rep rows 1–10 to form patt.

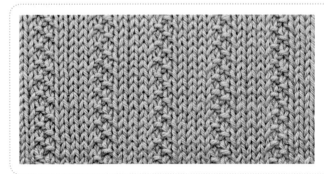

Seed Stitch Columns

Instructions

Cast on a multiple of 6sts plus 4 extra sts.
Row 1 (RS): K4, *k1, p1, k4, rep from * to end.
Row 2: *P5, k1, rep from * to last 4sts, p4.
Rep rows 1 and 2 to form patt.

Garter Rib

Instructions

Cast on a multiple of 8sts plus 4 extra sts.
Row 1 (RS): K4, *p4, k4, rep from * to end.
Row 2: P.
Rep rows 1 and 2 to form patt.

Basic Chevron

Instructions

Cast on a multiple of 12sts.
Row 1 (RS): *K2tog, k3, [inc in next st] twice, k3, s1 k1 psso, rep from * to end.
Row 2: P.
Rep rows 1 and 2 to form patt.

Garter Chevron

Instructions

Cast on a multiple of 11sts.
Row 1 (WS): K.
Rows 2, 3, 4, and 5: As row 1.
Row 6: *K2tog, k2, [inc in next st] twice, k3, s1 k1 psso, rep from * to end.
Row 7: P.
Rep last 2 rows twice more, then row 6 again.
Rep rows 1–12 to form patt.

Feather and Fan Stitch

Instructions

Cast on a multiple of 18sts plus 2 extra sts.
Row 1 (RS): K.
Row 2: P.
Row 3: K1, *[k2tog] three times, [yo, k1] six times, [k2tog] three times, rep from * to last st, k1.
Row 4: K.
Rep rows 1–4 to form patt.

2
Build On It

Having mastered the basics, it is time to move on and develop your knitting skills by learning how to manipulate fabrics into interesting shapes and twist stitches into decorative cables. And what you learned to do with two needles in the previous chapter, you can now apply to four or five needles. This chapter is all about shape and texture: you can practice the various techniques by making a variety of projects, from simple toys to stretchy, ribbed leg warmers and a chunky, cabled cushion.

Learn to knit:

Bunny Toy
pp.86–91

Leg Warmers
pp.96–99

Monkey Toy
pp.106–113

Cabled Cushion
pp.128–131

How to **Knit Simple Increases**

There are various ways of shaping a piece of knit fabric. This usually involves increasing (or decreasing) the number of stitches on the needle, either at the beginning, in the middle, or at the end of a row. Increasing the stitches can also be used to create texture and to form holes in openwork patterns.

Knit into front and back of stitch
(Abbreviation = *kfb* or *inc 1*)

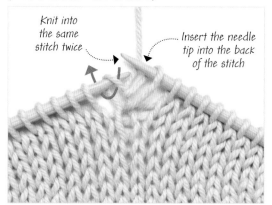

Knit into the same stitch twice

Insert the needle tip into the back of the stitch

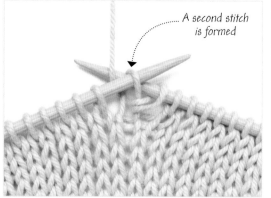

A second stitch is formed

1 Knit into the next stitch. Do not slip it off the needle but insert the tip of the right needle into the back of the same stitch, ready to knit into it again.

2 Wrap the yarn around the tip of the right needle, draw the yarn through to form a second stitch, then drop the old stitch off the left needle.

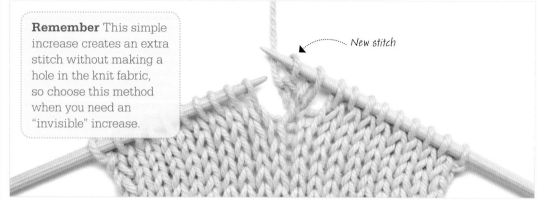

Remember This simple increase creates an extra stitch without making a hole in the knit fabric, so choose this method when you need an "invisible" increase.

New stitch

3 You will now have created two stitches out of one and you will have increased the number of stitches in the row by one.

This increase method is referred to as a "bar" increase, because it creates a horizontal bar below the new stitch.

Purl into front and back of stitch

(Abbreviation = *pfb* or *inc 1*)

Yarn from ball

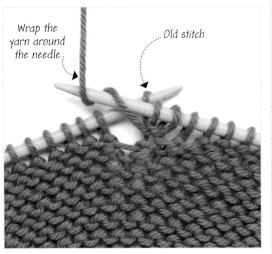

Wrap the yarn around the needle

Old stitch

1 When working on the purl side, purl the next stitch. Do not slip it off the needle but insert the tip of the right needle into the back of the loop from left to right.

2 Wrap the yarn around the tip of the right needle, draw the yarn through to form a second stitch, then drop the old stitch off the left needle.

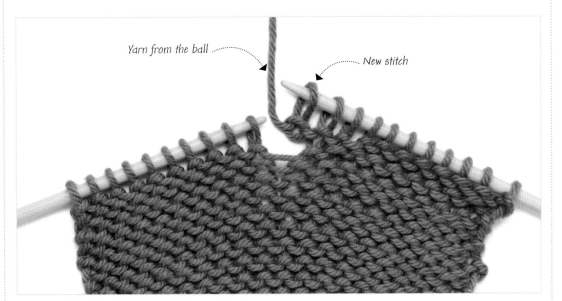

Yarn from the ball

New stitch

3 You have now created two stitches out of one and increased the number of stitches in the row by one.

Make-one left-leaning increase on a knit row

(Abbreviation = *M1 or M1k*)

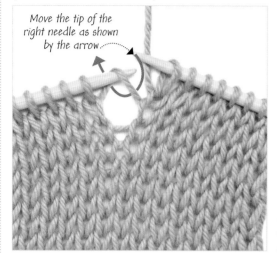

Move the tip of the right needle as shown by the arrow.

Knit into the back of the loop

1 Insert the tip of the left needle from front to back under the horizontal strand between the stitch just worked and insert the right needle into the back of this lifted loop.

2 Wrap the yarn around the tip of the right needle and draw the yarn through the lifted loop and then onto the right needle.

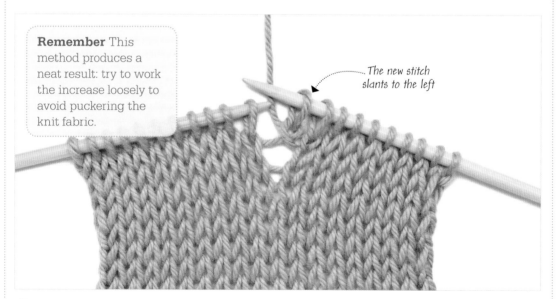

Remember This method produces a neat result: try to work the increase loosely to avoid puckering the knit fabric.

The new stitch slants to the left

3 You have now created an extra stitch in the row. Because you have knit through the back of the lifted loop, the base of the new stitch is twisted, minimizing any gap in the knitting that it might have created.

Make-one increase on purl row

(Abbreviation = *M1 or M1p*)

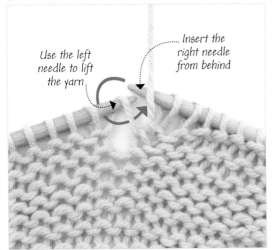

Use the left needle to lift the yarn

Insert the right needle from behind

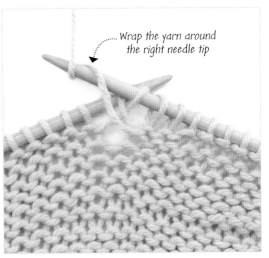

Wrap the yarn around the right needle tip

1 Use the left needle to lift the horizontal strand of yarn between the last stitch worked and the next stitch and insert the right needle from behind, left to right.

2 Wrap the yarn around the tip of the right needle and draw it through. This is called "purling through the back of the loop" and it twists the base of the new stitch.

Why? This simple increase method can cause a hole in the fabric. Knitting into the back of the loop twists the stitch and minimizes the hole.

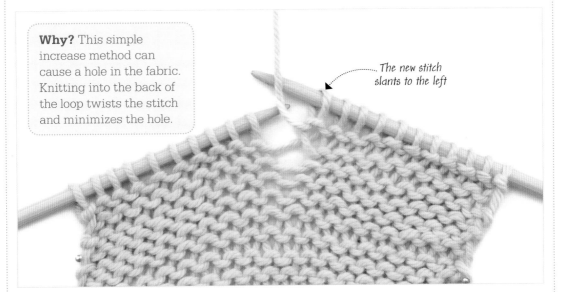

The new stitch slants to the left

3 You have now created an extra stitch from the strand of yarn between two stitches and increased the number of stitches in the row by one. The pattern instruction for this type of increase is "M1p" and it creates a tiny hole, but it is virtually invisible.

How to **Knit Yarn-over Increases**

You can form increases by creating extra loops of yarn (see pp.72–75). The method shown here creates a hole as well as a new stitch, so is referred to as a "visible" increase. The increases are usually placed carefully so that the holes form a pattern (see Hexagon and Square with Openwork, pp.104–105).

Yarn over between knit stitches

(Abbreviation = *yo*)

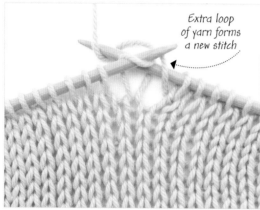

Extra loop of yarn forms a new stitch

Yarn from the ball

Right leg of the yarn-over loop is at the front

1 Bring the yarn to the front between the needles, then insert the right needle tip into the next stitch. Take the yarn over (yo) the top of the right needle and knit the stitch.

2 Drop the old stitch off the needle. You will now have two new stitches on the right needle, the first of these being formed by the yarn-over loop.

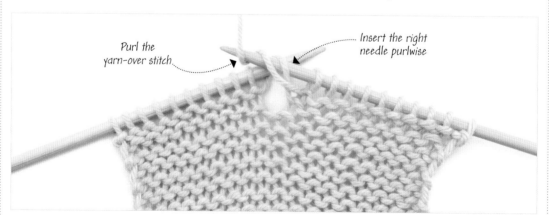

Purl the yarn-over stitch

Insert the right needle purlwise

3 On the following (purl) row, when you reach the stitch formed by the yarn over, purl it by inserting the right needle through the front loop from right to left, in the usual way. This will create an open hole under the purl stitch.

Yarn over between purl stitches

(Abbreviation = *yo*)

An extra loop is created by the yarn over

New stitch

1 Bring the yarn to the back of the work over the right needle, then to the front between the needles. Work the next purl stitch in the usual way (see p.41).

2 When you have completed the purl stitch, the yarn over will form a new stitch on the right needle with the right leg of the loop at the front.

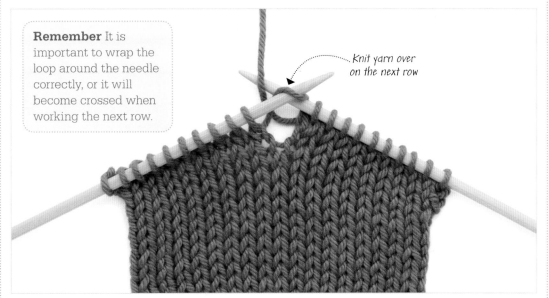

Remember It is important to wrap the loop around the needle correctly, or it will become crossed when working the next row.

Knit yarn over on the next row

3 On the following (knit) row, when you reach the stitch formed by the yarn over, knit it by inserting the right needle through the front loop from left to right and through the center of the stitch in the usual way. This will create an open hole below the knit stitch.

Yarn over between knit and purl stitches

(Abbreviation = *yo*)

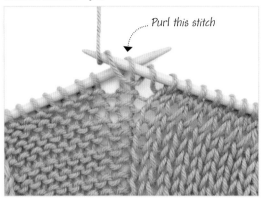

Purl this stitch

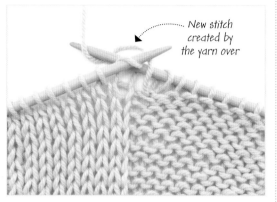

New stitch created by the yarn over

AFTER A KNIT STITCH AND BEFORE A PURL STITCH

After a knit stitch and before a purl stitch, bring the yarn to the front between the needles then over the top of the right needle and to the front again, then purl the next stitch.

AFTER A PURL STITCH AND BEFORE A KNIT STITCH

After a purl stitch and before a knit stitch, take the yarn over the top of the right needle to the back of the work, then knit the next stitch.

Yarn over at the beginning of a row

(Abbreviation = US *yo*; UK *yfwd* and *yrn*)

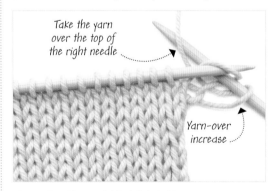

Take the yarn over the top of the right needle

Yarn-over increase

Yarn-over increase

AT THE BEGINNING OF A ROW BEFORE A KNIT STITCH

At the beginning of a knit row, with the yarn at the front, insert the tip of the right needle behind the yarn and into the first stitch, then take the yarn over the tip of the right needle to the back and complete the stitch.

AT THE BEGINNING OF A ROW BEFORE A PURL STITCH

Wrap the yarn from front to back over the top of the right needle, then to the front again between the needles; purl the first stitch. At the end of the next row, knit this new stitch in the usual way.

Double yarn over

(Abbreviation = *yo2* or *yo twice*)

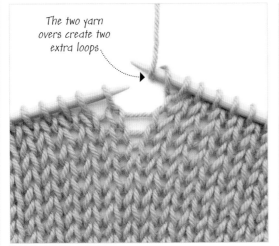

The two yarn overs create two extra loops.

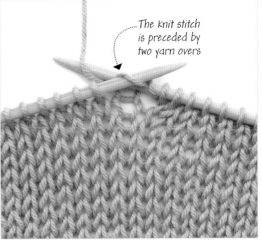

...The knit stitch is preceded by two yarn overs

1 Bring the yarn to the front, then over the top of the right needle to the back of the work, then between the needles to the front, then over the top of the right needle to the back.

2 Knit the next stitch in the usual way. There will be two extra loops on the right needle created by the double yarn over.

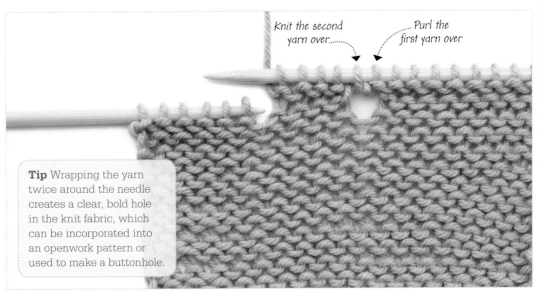

Knit the second yarn over.........   ...Purl the first yarn over

Tip Wrapping the yarn twice around the needle creates a clear, bold hole in the knit fabric, which can be incorporated into an openwork pattern or used to make a buttonhole.

3 On the following (purl) row, purl the first yarn over and knit the second. This will create an open hole below the stitches. As you are purling into loops, rather than fully-formed stitches, be careful that one of them doesn't slide off the needle.

How to **Knit Simple Decreases**

Decreasing is used for shaping pieces of knitting, for example at the top of a sleeve or along a neckline. Paired with increases, decreases can be used to create texture and lacy, openwork effects. This section shows you four ways to decrease a single stitch, and three ways to decrease two stitches; your pattern will tell you which of the methods to use.

Knit two together
(Abbreviation = *k2tog* or *dec 1*)

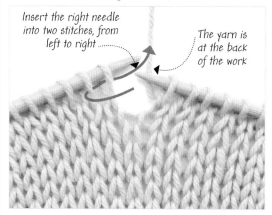

Insert the right needle into two stitches, from left to right ....

The yarn is at the back of the work

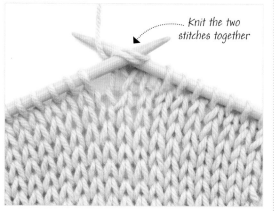

Knit the two stitches together

1 To knit two stitches together (k2tog), insert the tip of the right needle from left to right into the next two stitches on the left needle (into the second stitch, then the first).

2 Wrap the yarn around the tip of the right needle, draw the yarn through both loops, then drop both the old stitches off the left needle.

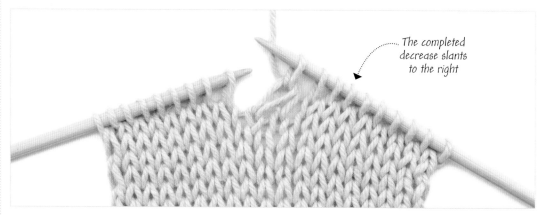

The completed decrease slants to the right

3 The two stitches, knit together, become one new stitch. This reduces the number of stitches in the row by one. Below the new stitch on the right needle you will now see that the decrease creates a right slant.

Purl two together

(Abbreviation = *p2tog* or *dec 1*)

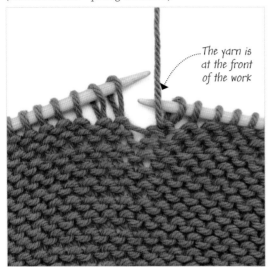

The yarn is at the front of the work

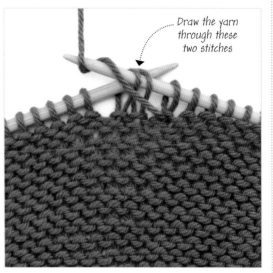

Draw the yarn through these two stitches

1 To purl two stitches together (p2tog), insert the tip of the right needle from right to left (purlwise) into the first two stitches on the left needle.

2 Wrap the yarn around the tip of the right needle, then draw it through both stitch loops and drop the two old stitches off the left needle.

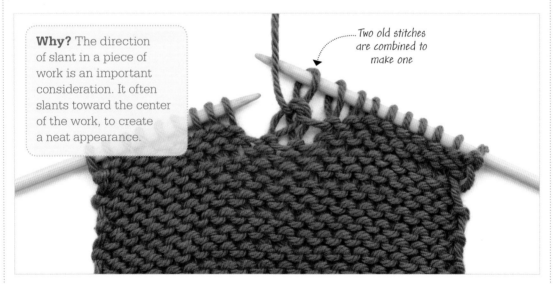

Why? The direction of slant in a piece of work is an important consideration. It often slants toward the center of the work, to create a neat appearance.

Two old stitches are combined to make one

3 The two old stitches have now been combined together to make one stitch and reduce the number of stitches in the row by one. The completed decrease slants to the right on the right side of the fabric.

Slip one, knit one, pass slipped stitch over

(Abbreviation = *s1 k1 psso* or *skp*)

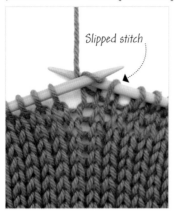

Slipped stitch

Pass the slipped stitch over the knit stitch

The completed decrease slants to the left

1 Insert the right needle into the next stitch and slip it knitwise (see p.134) on to the right needle. Knit the next stitch.

2 With the tip of the left needle, pick up the slipped stitch, lift it and pass it over the knit stitch and off the right needle.

3 You will now have reduced the number of stitches in the row by one and created a left slant decrease.

Slip, slip, knit

(Abbreviation = *ssk*)

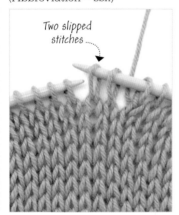

Two slipped stitches

Insert the left needle through the slipped stitches

The completed decrease slants to the left

1 Insert the right needle into the next two stitches from right to left and slip them knitwise (see p.134) on to the right needle.

2 Insert the tip of the left needle from left to right through the fronts of the two slipped stitches and knit these two stitches together.

3 You now have made one stitch from the previous two stitches and reduced the number of stitches in the row by one.

Double decreases

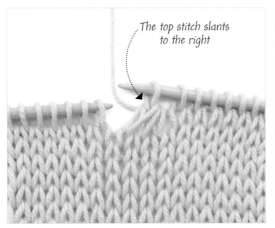

The top stitch slants to the right

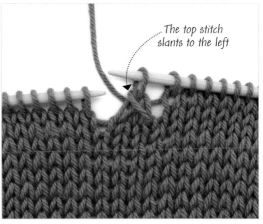

The top stitch slants to the left

k3tog

Where a pattern asks you to knit three stitches together (k3tog), insert the right needle tip from left to right into the next three stitches on the left needle and knit them together.

sl k2tog psso

Where a pattern instructions say "s1 k2tog psso," slip one stitch knitwise (see p.134) on to the right needle, knit the next two stitches together, then pass the slipped stitch over.

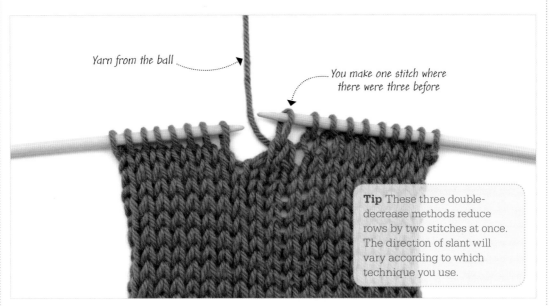

Yarn from the ball

You make one stitch where there were three before

> **Tip** These three double-decrease methods reduce rows by two stitches at once. The direction of slant will vary according to which technique you use.

s2k kl p2sso

Where a pattern instructs you to "s2k k1 p2sso," slip two stitches together knitwise on to the right needle, knit the next stitch, then pass the two slipped stitches together over the knit stitch and off the right needle. This creates a right slant decrease.

How to **Make Pom-poms**

Pom-poms are a classic embellishment for the top of a wool hat or the ends of tie cords. They can also be used, singly or in clusters, to decorate housewares such as cushions, tea cozies, and lamp shades. They are also a great way to use up all those odds and ends of yarn you have left over from knitting projects.

Cereal-box cardboard is the correct thickness for circle templates

The skein needs to fit through the holes in the cardboard

1 Cut out two cardboard circles, 3¼in (8 cm) in diameter, then cut out a 1 in (2.5 cm) hole from the center of each. Wind yarn into a small skein and, placing the cardboard rings together, wind the yarn around them, by inserting the skein through the hole.

Snip through the loops of yarn

Continue winding until the cardboard rings are thickly covered

2 When the first small skein of yarn runs out, make another and continue to cover the rings. If the hole becomes very small, use a blunt needle threaded with yarn to continue. Insert the scissor blades under the yarn loops at the perimeter and cut through.

Separate the cardboard rings

Tie the ends tightly

Wrap a double length of yarn around the bundle

3 Continue cutting through the loops all around the perimeter; pull the cardboard circles apart very slightly. Cut a double strand of yarn and slip it between the cardboard rings, wrap it around the core, and tie tightly in a knot to secure the bundle of yarn.

Trim the ends of the yarn to neaten the shape

Leave a yarn tail for attaching the pom-pom

Tip Cut larger or smaller cardboard rings for different sizes of pom-pom. The width of the ring (total diameter minus the hole diameter) decides the pom-pom size.

4 Thread the long yarn ends into a needle and sew through the knot at the center of the bundle to make it really secure, then remove the cardboard rings. Trim the pom-pom, leaving one long strand that can be used to attach it to your project.

Make a Bunny Toy

This pear-shaped rabbit is designed to help you practice simple increases and decreases to produce a three-dimensioned object. It also involves some simple embroidery and a few seams, to test your sewing skills.

Instructions

Difficulty Level
Moderate

Size
5 in (12 cm) tall

Yarn

Blue colorway
Rowan Wool Cotton 50 g
A: 968 Cypress x 1   B: 941 Clear x 1

Pink colorway
Rowan Wool Cotton 50 g
A: 943 Flower x 1   B: 951 Tender x 1

Needles
1 pair of US2 (3 mm/UK11) needles

Notions
Polyester toy stuffing
Dried chickpeas
      for stuffing
Blunt tapestry needle
Short length of black yarn
      for embroidery

Gauge
30 sts and 37 rows to 4 in (10 cm)
      over st st on US2 (3 mm/UK11)
      needles

**951
Tender x 1**

**968
Cypress x 1**

**941
Clear x 1**

**943
Flower x 1**

1 pair of US2 (3 mm/UK11) needles

Pattern
Body
Using yarn A, cast on 16 sts,
placing a marker at center of
cast-on edge.
Row 1: Inc1 in every st to end.
(32 sts)
Row 2 and all foll alt rows: P.
Row 3: [K1, inc1 in next st] to end.
(48 sts)
Row 5: [K2, inc1 in next st] three
times, k to last 7 sts, [inc1 in next
st, k2] twice, inc1 in last st. (54 sts)
Row 7: K.
Row 9: [K3, inc1 in next st] three
times, [k2, inc1 in next st] to last

12 sts, [inc1 in next st, k3] to end.
(70 sts)
Row 11: K.
Row 13: [K4, inc1 in next st] three
times, k to last 16 sts, [inc1 in next
st, k4] twice, inc1 in last st. (76 sts)
Work 13 rows without shaping.

Shape Back
Row 1: [K3, k2tog] six times,
k to last 27 sts, [k2tog, k3] five
times, k2tog. (64 sts)
Work 3 rows without shaping.
Row 5: [K2, k2tog] six times,
k to last 22 sts, [k2tog, k2] five
times, k2tog. (52 sts)
Next and all foll alt rows: P.

Row 7: [K1, k2tog] four times, k to
last 11 sts, [k2tog, k1] three times,
k2tog. (44 sts)
Row 9: K12, k2tog, k2, k2tog, k8,
k2tog, k2, k2tog, k to end. (40 sts)
Row 11: K1, k2tog, k to last 3 sts,
k2tog, k1. (38 sts)
Row 13: K10, k2tog, k2, k2tog, k6,
k2tog, k2, k2tog, k to end. (34 sts)
Row 15: K1, k2tog, k to last 3 sts,
k2tog, k1. (32 sts)
Work 7 rows without shaping.

Shape Head
Row 1: *K2, k2tog, rep from *
to end. (24 sts)
Row 2 and all foll alt rows: P.

Row 3: [K1, k2tog] to end. (16sts)
Row 5: [K2tog] to end. (8sts)
Using a tapestry needle, draw yarn
through rem sts twice. Join row
ends to form back seam, using
mattress stitch (see p.44) and leave
the bottom open. Stuff firmly with
toy stuffing, inserting a layer of
dried chickpeas at the base of the
bunny. Line up back seam with
marker at bunny's front and squash
flat. Whip stitch this seam together.
For the tail, make a 1¼in (3cm)
pom-pom (see pp.84–85) from
yarn B. Using picture as a guide,
affix to the back of the bunny.

Spots (Make 3)

Using yarn B, cast on 3sts.
Row 1: K.
Row 2: Inc1 in first st, p1, inc1
in last st. (5sts)
Row 3: K.
Row 4: P.
Row 5: K.
Row 6: P2tog, p1, p2tog. (3sts)
Row 7: K.
Cast off, leaving a long tail of yarn.
Arrange spots randomly on the
bunny's body and, using long tail
of yarn, oversew to secure.

Feet (Make 2)

Using yarn A, cast on 6sts.
Row 1: K.
Row 2: P.
Rep last 2 rows five times more.
Cast off. With RS facing, sew
cast-on and cast-off edge together
(see p.44). This seam forms the
back of the foot. Using picture
as a guide, pin feet in place and
stitch to underside of body.

Ears (Make 2)

Using yarn A, cast on 6sts and
work 10 rows st st.
Next row (RS): K1, s1 k1 psso,
k2tog, k1. (4sts)

Next row: P. Change to yarn B.
Next row: K2, M1, k2. (5sts)
Beginning with a p row, work 9
rows st st. Cast off. Fold ear piece
in half to match cast-on to cast-off
edge. Join row ends and stitch in

*Fold one ear over
for a cute,
lopsided effect*

position. If you want, bring an ear
down with a single stitch to affix
to the head for a lopsided, cute
look. Then sew on eyes (see p.91).
Using black yarn, embroider nose
in satin stitch (see p.90).

*Make the spots
separately and
stitch them to
the sides*

Adding weight

Fill the finished bunny with a lightweight, polyester toy stuffing, adding a handful of dried chickpeas for weight. This will help the bunny to sit upright.

Pom-pom tail

As a fluffy tail, a pom-pom is ideal. You will find instructions for making one on pp.84–85. Remember to leave a long tail of yarn for sewing the finished pom-pom into place.

Embroider the features on the stockinette stitch base (see pp.90–91)

Use spare yarn to make a pom-pom tail

Make the feet separately and sew them to the base

How to **Embroider on Knit**

There are various embroidery stitches that can be used to embellish knit fabrics and to add simple decorative details such as facial features. To stitch these, use a blunt-ended tapestry needle and choose a yarn of a similar weight to the one you have used for knitting, or very slightly thicker.

Duplicate stitch vertical

Duplicate stitch is called this, because it mimics the rows of knit stitches.

1 Bring the needle to the front, through the center of a knit stitch, then insert it from right to left behind the stitch. Pull the yarn through.

2 Insert the needle under the top of the stitch below, up through the top of the stitch, emerging from the center of the stitch just covered.

Duplicate stitch horizontal

Here, Swiss darning is worked in horizontal rows, in a way similar to the vertical rows shown above.

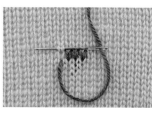

1 Bring the needle through to the front, through the center of a knit stitch. Insert it, right to left, behind the stitch. Pull the yarn through.

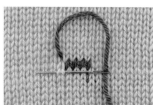

2 Insert the needle, right to left, in knit stitch below, out through the center of the next knit stitch to the left: follow the path of the row of stitches.

Satin Stitch

Closely spaced, straight stitches are useful for filling in a simple shape.

1 Bring the needle to the front, between the knit stitches at one side of the intended shape. Take the needle back between two stitches on the other side.

2 Bring the needle to the front at the original side and make another stitch parallel to the first. The stitches should lie flat and close together.

Use satin stitch (see opposite) to embroider the nose

Embroider the mouth in backstitch (as in a backstitch seam, see p.45)

Make the eyes by embroidering with yarn B in satin stitch, then whip stitch with black yarn

How to **Knit in the Round**

To produce seamless knitting you need either a circular needle or a set of double-pointed needles. With the right side of the work always facing you, instead of "rows," you work in "rounds," usually resulting in a tube of knitting or a flat "medallion." It is easier than you might think: try it with a circular needle before going on to four or five double-pointed needles.

Working with a circular knitting needle

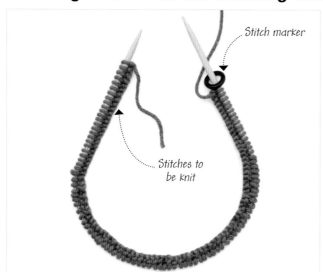

Stitch marker

Stitches to be knit

1 Cast on the required number of stitches using your preferred method. You must make sure that the line of stitches is not twisted and that the cast-on edge faces inward. Slip a stitch marker (or a knotted loop of contrast yarn) onto the right needle, to mark the beginning of the round.

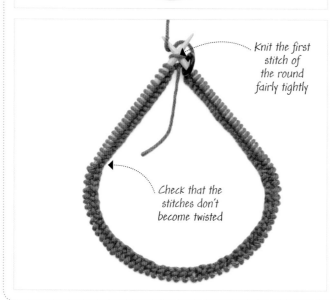

Knit the first stitch of the round fairly tightly

Check that the stitches don't become twisted

2 Hold the needle ends in your hands—just as you would when using two straight needles—and bring the right needle tip up to the left needle to work each stitch. When you reach the stitch marker, slip it from the left needle onto the right needle and continue knitting, trying to make sure you knit the first stitch of each round fairly tightly, to avoid leaving a gap in the stitches.

The wrong side of the work is always on the inside

Knit the first stitch of the round fairly tightly

3 If you are creating a fabric in stockinette stitch (see p.40), you would work one row knit, one row purl, on two straight needles. With a circular needle, you just continue every round in knit stitch. The right side of the work will always be facing you and every round will be a knit round.

> **Remember** Use a long circular needle to knit a large item such as the body of a sweater seamlessly; use shorter circular needles for smaller items such as a hat, bag, or neckband.

Joining the circle of stitches

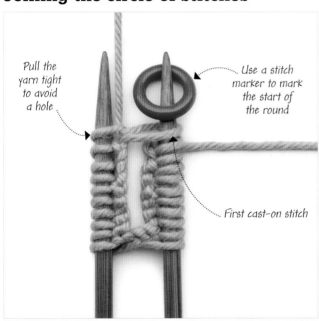

Pull the yarn tight to avoid a hole

Use a stitch marker to mark the start of the round

First cast-on stitch

For a neat finish, try this method of closing the circle in the first round of circular knitting. First, when you cast on, add an extra stitch, then transfer the first cast-on stitch from the left needle on to the right needle, next to the last cast-on stitch, and place a stitch marker on the needle. Knit the round and, when you reach the end, knit the last two stitches together before the marker.

How to **Work with Double-pointed Needles**

Knitting on double-pointed needles is similar to working on a circular needle, since you work in rounds. Although slightly trickier to manipulate, double-pointed needles (referred to in patterns as "dpns") are more versatile—you can work with very few stitches, which allows you to knit seamless gloves and socks and to produce flat "medallions."

Working with a set of four double-pointed needles

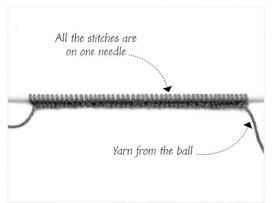

All the stitches are on one needle

Yarn from the ball

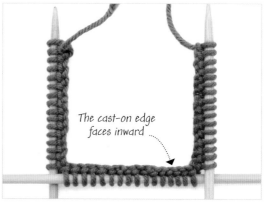

The cast-on edge faces inward

1 When working with a set of four double-pointed needles, begin by casting on the required number of stitches on just one of the needles.

2 Distribute your stitches onto three of the needles and use the fourth for knitting. Make sure the stitches are not twisted: the base of each stitch should face inward.

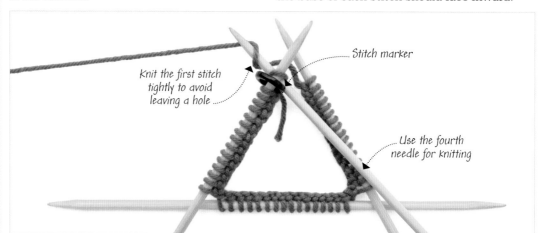

Knit the first stitch tightly to avoid leaving a hole

Stitch marker

Use the fourth needle for knitting

3 Place a stitch marker between the first and second stitches on the first needle, to mark the beginning of the round. Then pull the tips of the first and third needles together (with the second needle forming the base of the triangle) and start to knit using the fourth.

Working with a set of five double-pointed needles

Make sure the stitches are not twisted

Stitch marker

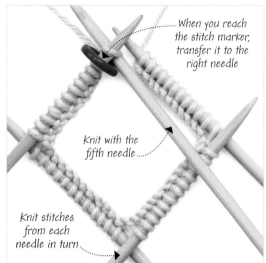

When you reach the stitch marker, transfer it to the right needle

Knit with the fifth needle

Knit stitches from each needle in turn

1 Just as you do when using four needles, cast on the required number of stitches onto one needle, then distribute the stitches, this time between four of the needles.

2 Once you have arranged all the stitches on the four needles, begin to knit using the fifth needle. Knit the first stitch tightly, to avoid a hole.

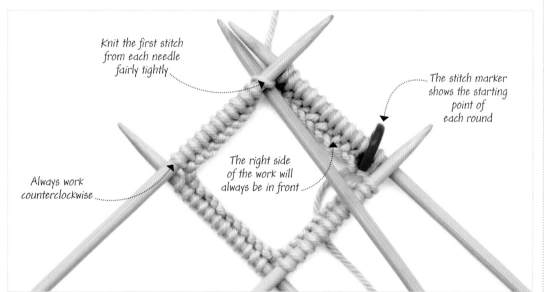

Knit the first stitch from each needle fairly tightly

The stitch marker shows the starting point of each round

Always work counterclockwise

The right side of the work will always be in front

3 To complete a round of knitting, first knit all the stitches from the first needle, then use this needle (which is now empty of stitches) to do the knitting. When you reach the end of the round, slip the stitch marker from the left to the right needle.

Leg Warmers

Worked in knit one, purl one rib, instructions are given here for both seamless leg warmers knit in the round on four double-pointed needles, and for ones that can be knit on two regular needles and seamed afterward. The choice is yours.

Instructions

Difficulty Level
Easy

Size
One size fits all, 22 in (55 cm) long

Yarn
Berroco Peruvia 100 g
7175 Rio x 4

Needles
A: Set of four US5 (3.75 mm/UK9)
double-pointed needles, or
B: 1 pair of US5 (3.75 mm/UK9)
needles
C: Set of four US6 (4 mm/UK8)
double-pointed needles, or
D: 1 pair of US6 (4 mm/UK8) needles

Gauge
22 sts and 30 rows to 4 in (10 cm)
over st st on US6 (4 mm/UK8)
needles

Notions
Blunt tapestry needle

**7175
Rio x 3**

US5 (3.75 mm/UK9) needles

US6 (4 mm/UK8) needles

Pattern

In the round (make 2)
With US5 (3.75 mm/UK9) double-
pointed needles (A), cast on 60 sts
and distribute them evenly
between 3 needles.
Work in rounds of k1, p1 rib for
2¼ in (5 cm).
Change to US6 (4 mm/UK8)
double-pointed needles (C) and
cont in rib until your work
measures 20 in (50 cm) from beg.
Change back to needles A and rib
a further 2¼ in (5 cm). Cast off
in rib.

With seam (make 2)
With US5 (3.75 mm/UK9) needles
(B), cast on 60 sts.
Work in k1, p1 rib for 2¼ in (5 cm).

Change to US6 (4 mm/UK8)
needles (D) and cont in rib until
work measures 20 in (50 cm) from
beg.
Change back to needles B, and
rib for another 2¼ in (5 cm).
Cast off in rib.
Join back leg seam, using
mattress stitch (see p.44).

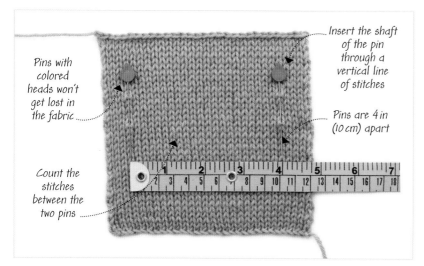

Pins with colored heads won't get lost in the fabric

Insert the shaft of the pin through a vertical line of stitches

Pins are 4 in (10 cm) apart

Count the stitches between the two pins

To increase the length of the leg warmers, simply continue the rib pattern

Checking gauge

Make sure you are knitting to the correct gauge to keep the leg warmers from being too loose or too tight. Knit a sample swatch in stockinette stitch and measure to check there are 22 stitches and 30 rows to a 4 in (10 cm) square (see p.140).

Single Rib

The leg warmers shown here are knit in single rib (see p.64). Both double- and single-rib fabrics are reversible and do not curl at the edges.

Tip When casting on, using the long-tail cast-on technique (see p.38) will give a firm, elastic edge. To keep the ribbed corrugations, cast off in rib (see below) for more "stretch."

Ribbing (formed by knitting and purling alternate stitches) creates a double-sided fabric

Casting off in rib effect

Pass first stitch over the second

1 Work a k1, p1 sequence: with the yarn to the back, insert the left needle into the first stitch. Pass it over the second stitch and off the right needle.

2 Knit the next stitch. Pass the first stitch over the second and off the right needle as before.

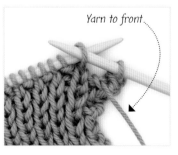

Yarn to front

3 Take the yarn to the front and purl the next stitch. Repeat steps 1 and 2 until the row is complete, pulling the last stitch through itself to finish.

How to **Work a Simple Square**

Knit medallions are simple shapes knit on multiple needles and worked from the center outward. The step-by-step instructions on these pages show you how to work a square—but the principle of working in rounds with regular increases is the same for circles, hexagons, octagons, and other similar flat geometric shapes.

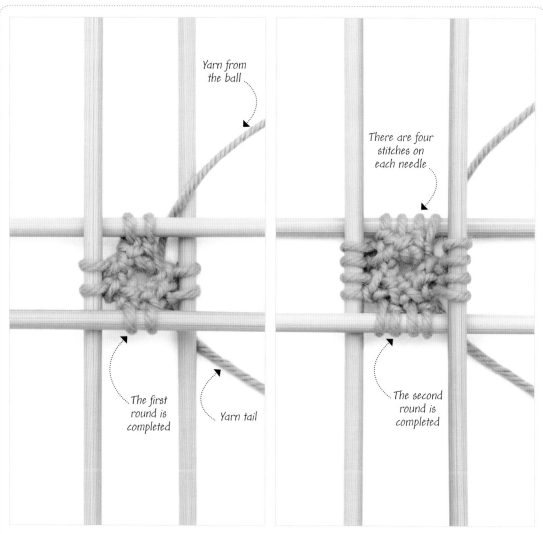

Yarn from the ball

There are four stitches on each needle

The first round is completed

Yarn tail

The second round is completed

1 Cast on eight stitches and distribute them between four double-pointed needles—two stitches on each. Using a fifth needle to knit with, knit through the back loop of each stitch.

2 For round 2, you will need to make eight increases: to do this, knit into the front and back of each stitch; you will now have a total of 16 stitches, four on each needle.

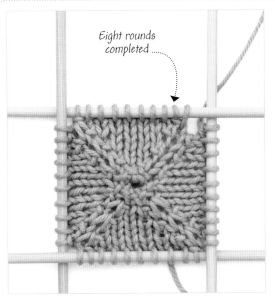

Eight rounds completed ......

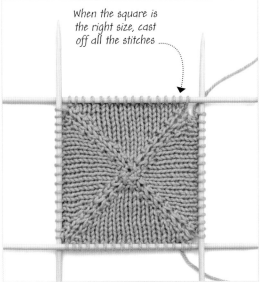

When the square is the right size, cast off all the stitches ......

3 For round 3, knit each stitch. For round 4, make eight increases: knit into the front and back of the first and last stitches on each needle. Rounds 5-8: repeat rounds 3–4 twice.

4 Continue in this way, adding eight stitches on every other round, increasing in the first and last stitch on each needle. Keep on until your square is the desired size.

Leave a long yarn tail ......

5 Cut the yarn, leaving a tail. Using a blunt needle, pass the tail under the top of the first cast-off stitch and back through the center of the fastened-off stitch. Darn in the ends.

Uses for your shapes

To make a pot holder, use a cotton yarn and just keep knitting, following the instructions in step 4, until your square is the desired size.

Make a four-square cushion cover by joining four square medallions of equal size. The squares may all be the same color, or you could make two squares in each of two colors, or each square in a different color.

For a plain cushion, knit two identical square medallions for the front and back of the cushion. When making large medallions, you will need to use longer double-pointed needles to accommodate the extra stitches.

Create a patchwork throw by joining together a number of square medallions, interspersed with plain knit squares, or squares knit in one or more of the simple textured stitches shown on pp.64–69.

How to **Knit Medallions**

The method of knitting a square medallion, described on pp.100-101, applies, with a few variations, to any flat shape knit in the round. You will find full pattern instructions on pp.104–105 for knitting some of the shapes described below—but once you have the hang of the basic concept, you could invent your own shapes and patterns.

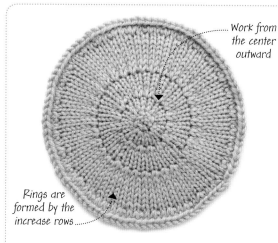

Work from the center outward

Rings are formed by the increase rows

Use the yarn end to close up the hole in the center

Use five double-pointed needles to knit a circle. Start by increasing in every stitch of the round, then in every second stitch, every third stitch, and so on, to create a flat disk.

To knit a square, you will need to use five needles. The method for making the square shown here is described on pp.100–101.

Yarn-over increases create a swirling pattern

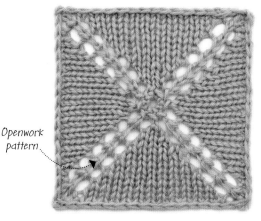

Openwork pattern

A variation of the plain square, these swirls are created by bringing the yarn forward to create an extra stitch (rather than by knitting into the front and back of a stitch).

The placement of yarn-over increases on this square creates attractive diagonal lines of openwork holes, forming a cross.

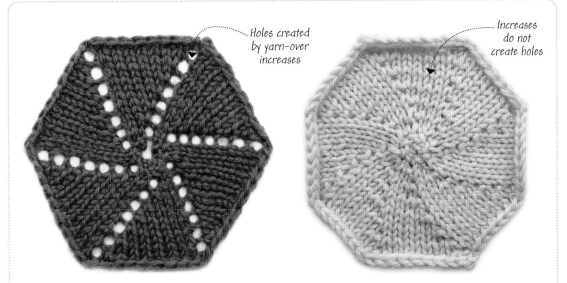

Holes created by yarn-over increases

Increases do not create holes

To knit a hexagonal shape, use four double-pointed needles. In this example, yarn-over increases create a pattern of openwork lines radiating out from the center of the shape.

Use five double-pointed needles for an octagon, and work eight increases on every round, by knitting into the front and back of stitches.

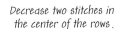

Decrease two stitches in the center of the rows

Instead of knitting in the round, this square is created on two needles, with the pattern of converging lines of stitches created by decreasing in the center of each row.

Uses for your shapes

To make a patchwork, join a number of similar, straight-sided shapes—such as squares, hexagons, or octagons. A few medallions will make a cushion cover, while a larger number might make a cover for a baby's crib or even a full-sized bedspread.

Coasters can be created from small medallions. Use remnants of fine cotton yarn and small needles. Circles, hexagons, or octagons are the best shapes for this purpose.

For a basket liner, any single medallion, knit in a crisp, cotton yarn, is ideal. Just choose the shape to match your basket and keep knitting until you have created a large enough shape.

To make a bag, use any medallion shape as a base. When your shape is the right size for the bag base, continue knitting in rounds, without increases, to form the bag's sides.

Gallery of **Shapes**

Most knitters begin by knitting with two needles, but once you have mastered the basics of working in rows, you can progress to using four or five double-pointed needles (dpns). This allows you to work in rounds, and opens up a new area of pattern possibilities, like these flat geometric shapes. So pick up those dpns and try them for yourself.

Simple Square

Instructions

Cast on 8sts on one needle. Then distribute 2sts on each of four double-pointed needles and knit with a 5th double-pointed needle as foll:
Round 1: [K1 tbl] twice on each of four needles.
Round 2: [Kfb in each st] on each of four needles. (16sts)
Round 3: K.

Round 4: [K, working kfb in first and last st] on each of four needles. (24sts)
Rep rounds 3 and 4 (increasing 8sts in every alt round) until square is desired size.
Cast off knitwise.

Square with Swirl Increases

Instructions

Cast on 8sts on one needle. Then distribute 2sts on each of four double-pointed needles, and knit with a 5th double-pointed needle as foll:
Row 1: [K1 tbl] twice on each of four needles.

Row 2: [K, working yo before first st] on each of four needles. (12sts)
Rep round 2 (increasing 4sts in every round) until square is desired size.
Cast off knitwise.

Hexagon

Instructions

Cast on 12sts on one needle. Then distribute 4sts on each of three double-pointed needles and knit with a 4th double-pointed needle as foll:
Round 1: [K1 tbl] four times on each of three needles.
Round 2: [Yo, k2, yo, k2] on each needles. (18sts)
Round 3: K on each of three needles.

Round 4: [Yo, k3, yo, k3] on each of three needles. (24sts)
Round 5: K.
Round 6: [Yo, k half of rem sts on needle, yo, k to end of needle] on each of three needles. (30sts)
Rep rounds 5 and 6 (increasing 6sts in every alt round) until hexagon is desired size.
Cast off knitwise.

Simple Circle

Instructions

Cast on 8sts on one needle. Then distribute 2sts on each of four double-pointed needles and knit with a 5th double-pointed needle as foll:
Round 1: [K1 tbl] twice on each of four needles.
Round 2: [Kfb in each st] on each of four needles. (16sts)
Rounds 3, 4, and 5: K.
Round 6: [Kfb in each st] on each of four needles. (32sts)
Rounds 7, 8, 9, 10, and 11: K.
Round 12: Rep round 6. (64sts)
Rounds 13, 14, 15, 16, 17, 18, and 19: K.

Round 20: [Kfb into every 2nd st] on each of four needles. (96sts)
Rounds 21, 22, 23, 24, and 25: K.
Round 26: [Kfb into every 3rd st] on each of four needles. (128sts)
Rounds 27, 28, 29, 30, and 31: K.
Round 32: [Kfb into every 4th st] on each of four needles. (160sts)
Cont in this way, increasing 32 stitches in every 6th round and working the next increase round with kfb into every 5th stitch, the following into every 6th stitch, and so on, until the circle is the desired size.
Cast off knitwise.

Simple Octagon

Instructions

Cast on 8sts on one needle. Then distribute 2sts on each of four double-pointed needles and knit with a 5th double-pointed needle as foll:
Round 1: [K1 tbl] twice on each of four needles.
Round 2: [Kfb in each st] on each of four needles. (16sts)
Round 3 and all odd-numbered rounds: K.
Round 4: [K1, kfb, k1, kfb] on each of four needles. (24sts)

Round 6: [K2, kfb, k2, kfb] on each of four needles. (32sts)
Round 8: [K3, kfb, k3, kfb] on each of four needles. (40sts)
Round 10: [K4, kfb, k4, kfb] on each of four needles. (48sts)
Round 12: [K5, kfb, k5, kfb] on each of four needles. (56sts)
Cont in this way (increasing 8sts in every alt round) until octagon is desired size.
Cast off knitwise.

Square with Openwork

Instructions

Cast on 8sts on one needle. Then distribute 2sts on each of four double-pointed needles and knit with a 5th double-pointed needle as foll:
Round 1: [K1 tbl] twice on each of four needles.
Round 2: [Yo, k1, yo, k1] on each of four needles. (16sts)
Round 3: K.
Round 4: [Yo, k2, yo, k1] on each of four needles. (24sts)

Round 5: K.
Round 6: [Yo, k to last st, yo, k1] on each of four needles. (32sts)
Rep rounds 5 and 6 (increasing 8sts in every alt round) until square is desired size.
Cast off knitwise.

Make a Monkey Toy

If you have never made a toy before, this is a good place to start. Knit in sections, using your own choice of yarn, this monkey gives you lots of opportunities to practice following a pattern, changing colors, seaming, stuffing, assembling, attaching buttons, and embroidering.

Instructions

Difficulty Level
Moderate

Size
Variable
(see Yarns and Needles box, below)

Yarn
Lightweight or medium-weight
yarn in six pastel colors:
A: turquoise, B: mint green,
C: lavender, D: pale lilac,
E: pale green, F: pale pink
(see Yarns and Needles box, below)

Needles
1 pair of needles
(see Yarns and Needles box, below)

Notions
Polyester toy stuffing
Blunt tapestry needle
2 plastic buttons
Sewing needles and thread
Embroidery thread, in black

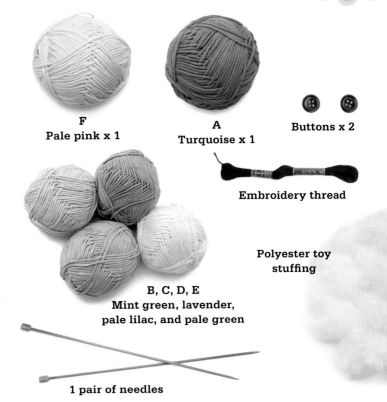

F
Pale pink x 1

A
Turquoise x 1

Buttons x 2

Embroidery thread

**Polyester toy
stuffing**

B, C, D, E
**Mint green, lavender,
pale lilac, and pale green**

1 pair of needles

Pattern
Body and head
Work the body and head in one
piece, starting at the lower end.
Using one of the stripe colors (B, C,
D, or E), cast on 20sts, leaving
a long tail for the back seam.
Row 1 (RS): [Kfb, k1] 10 times.
(30sts)
Row 2: P.
Row 3: K1, [M1, K3] 9 times, M1,
k2. (40sts)
Row 4: P.
Row 5: K2, [M1, K4] 9 times, M1,
k2. (50sts)
Cont in st st in random stripes for
13 more rows, ending with RS
facing for next row.
Next row (RS): K6, [k2tog, k10] 3
times, k2tog, k6. (46sts)
Next row: P.
Next row: K1, [k2tog, k4] 7 times,
k2tog, k1. (38sts)

Next row: P.

Next row: K3, [k2tog, k8] 3 times, k2tog, k3. (34sts)

Next row: P.

Next row: K4, [k2tog, k3] 6 times. (28sts)

Work 9 rows without shaping, ending with RS facing for next row.

Shape shoulders

Next row (RS): K6, k2tog, k12, k2tog, k6. (26sts)

Next row: P.

Next row: K5, s1 k2tog psso, k10, s1 k2tog psso, k5. (22sts)

Next row: P.

Next row: K4, s1 k2tog psso, k8, s1 k2tog psso, k4. (18sts)

Next row: P.

Head

Next row (RS): K2, [kfb, k1] 8 times. (26sts)

Next row: P.

Next row: K2, [M1, k3] 8 times. (34sts)

Next row: P.

Next row: K4, [M1, k5] 6 times. (40sts)

Work 17 rows without shaping, ending with RS facing for next row.

Next row: K2 [k2tog, k3] 7 times, k2tog, k1. (32sts)

Next row: P.

Next row: K1, [k2tog, k2] 7 times, k2tog, k1. (24sts)

Next row: P.

Next row: [K2tog, k1] 8 times. (16sts)

Next row: P.

Next row: [K2tog] 8 times. (8sts)

Next row: [P2tog] 4 times. (4sts)

Cut off yarn, leaving a long tail. Thread tail onto a blunt-ended yarn needle and pass needle through 4 rem sts as they are dropped from needle. Pull yarn to gather, and secure with a few stitches.

Legs (make 2)

Each leg is started at the foot end. Using A (foot and hand color), cast on 6sts using the backward loop cast-on method (see p.37) and leaving a long tail.

Row 1 (RS): [Kfb] 5 times, k1. (11sts)

Row 2: P.

Row 3: K1, [M1, k1] 10 times. (21sts)

Beg with a P row, work 9 rows in st st, ending with RS facing for next row.

Row 13 (RS): K2, [k2tog, k3] 3 times, k2tog, k2. (17sts)

Row 14: P.

Cut off A.

Cont in st st in random stripes (of B, C, D, and E) throughout as follows:

Work 10 rows without shaping, ending with RS facing for next row.

Next row (RS): K4, k2tog, k6, k2tog, k3. (15sts)

Work 15 rows without shaping.

Next row (RS): K3, [k2tog, k2] twice, k2tog, k2. (12sts)**

Work 11 rows without shaping. Cast off knitwise.

Arms (make 2)

Each arm is started at the hand end. Work as for leg to **.

Work seven rows without shaping. Cast off 2sts at beg of next 4 rows. Cast off rem 4sts, leaving a long tail for sewing arm to body.

Muzzle

Using one of the stripe colors (B, C, D, or E), cast on 6sts, using backward loop cast-on method (see p.37) and leaving a long tail.

Row 1 (RS): [Kfb] 5 times, k1. (11sts)

Row 2: P.

Row 3: K1, [M1, k1] 10 times. (21sts)

Row 4: P.

Cut off first stripe color and change to a second stripe color for remainder of muzzle.

Row 5: K1, [M1, k2] 10 times. (31sts)

Beg with a p row, work 5 rows in st st.

Cast off knitwise, leaving a long tail for sewing muzzle to body.

Ears (make 2)

Using F (ear and tail color), cast on 3 sts.

Row 1 (WS): [Kfb] twice, k1. (5sts)

Note: Work the remaining increases as yarn overs (see p.76), ensuring that each yarn over is crossed when it is knit in the following row, to close the hole by knitting it through the back of the loop.

Row 2 (RS): [K1, yo] 4 times, k1. (9sts)

Row 3: K to end, knitting each yo through back loop.

Row 4: [K2, yo] 4 times, k1. (13sts)

Row 5: Rep row 3.

Row 6: K.

Rows 7 and 8: K.

Cast off loosely knitwise, leaving a long tail for gathering ear into cupped shape and sewing to head.

Tail

Using F (ear and tail color), cast on 3sts, leaving a long tail for sewing tail to body.

Work in garter stitch (k every row) until tail is a little longer than leg (or desired length).

Next row: S1 k2tog psso, then fasten off.

Tail will twist naturally—do not press it.

Finishing

Make up the monkey following the instructions on pp.109–113.

1 When knitting the body and head, which are made in one piece, choose your own color combinations for the stripes, joining in new colors (see p.52) at the beginning of a row.

Remember Knit sections take on their final shape once they are stitched and stuffed, so do not be surprised if they look a bit shapeless at this early stage.

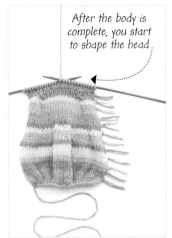

After the body is complete, you start to shape the head

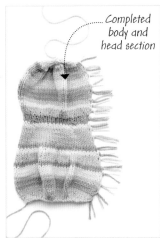

Completed body and head section

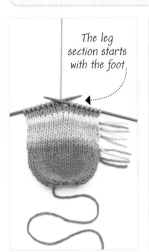

The leg section starts with the foot

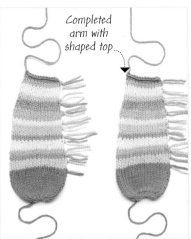

Completed arm with shaped top

2 After the body and head section, the next step is to knit the legs and arms. These are made starting with the foot or hand, working upward.

Careful! If the pattern instructs you to leave a long yarn tail at the beginning or end of a section, make sure you leave enough yarn—about 12 in (30 cm) should be adequate—to allow for gathering edges or sewing seams.

3 After the body and head, the legs, and the arms, there are still a few more pieces to knit. To shape the muzzle, the pattern instructions require you to employ both kfb and M1 increases (see p.72 and p.75).

Careful! Cast off the edge of the muzzle quite loosely, to leave a neat row of chain stitches, since this is the edge you will stitch to the front of the monkey's head.

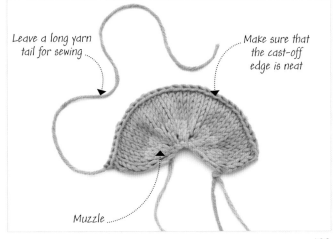

Leave a long yarn tail for sewing

Make sure that the cast-off edge is neat

Muzzle

4 In contrast to the stockinette stitch body, head, and legs, the tail and ears are worked in garter stitch (see p.40). The tail is a simple strip, while the ears involve a little bit of shaping.

Careful! Even if the instructions do not require you to leave a long yarn tail, you should not snip the yarn off too short, because you will need to thread it into a needle for weaving in neatly.

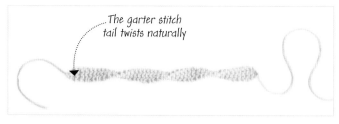
...The garter stitch tail twists naturally

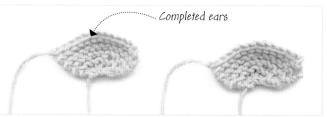
......Completed ears

.... Hide the short yarn tails on the inside

The mattress stitch seam is almost invisible

5 When you have finished knitting all the different components, it is time to start seaming and stuffing. Start with the legs, sewing the sides together using mattress stitch (see p.44), starting with the foot and working upward, adding stuffing as you go.

Careful! Stuff the legs firmly, but do not overly stuff or you will stretch and distort them.

6 It is easier to sew the button eyes in place before sewing the seam on the body and head. Place them three or four stitches apart, center front of the head.

Careful! If the toy is designed for a small child, you must sew on the button eyes very securely, or consider replacing them with snap-on safety eyes (available from craft suppliers), or with embroidered eyes instead.

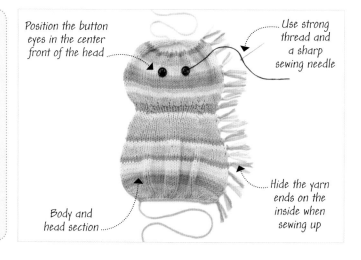
Position the button eyes in the center front of the head ....

...Use strong thread and a sharp sewing needle

Body and head section ......

Hide the yarn ends on the inside when sewing up

7 Starting at the base (the cast-on edge) and working upward, stitch about 1 in (2.5 cm) of the back seam using mattress stitch (see p.44). Then sew the cast-on edges together, to form the base, trapping the tops of the two legs inside this seam.

Remember When attaching the legs, make sure that the leg seams are at the back, because this will look much neater.

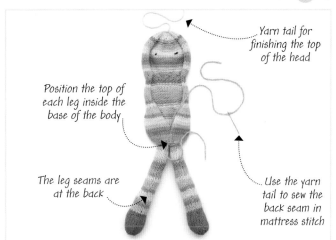

Yarn tail for finishing the top of the head

Position the top of each leg inside the base of the body

The leg seams are at the back

Use the yarn tail to sew the back seam in mattress stitch

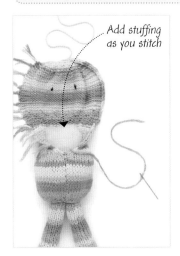

Add stuffing as you stitch

Stuff firmly, but be careful not to distort the shape

8 Continue sewing up the back seam using mattress stitch, adding stuffing and tucking in the yarn ends as you go.

Why? The reason for adding the stuffing in stages, as you sew up the back seam, is that it is easier to stuff the toy in sections than to wait until you reach the head. Otherwise, you will be left with only a small hole through which to poke the stuffing.

9 Prepare the arms in the same way as you did the legs, using a mattress-stitch seam. Stuff each arm, but do not stitch the tops of the arms closed.

Why? You need to leave the top of each arm open, since you will have to stitch it to the outside of the body. To do this neatly, it will be necessary to turn the cast-off edge to the inside, so that it does not create an unsightly ridge.

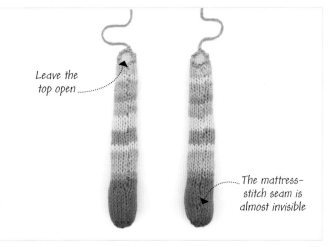

Leave the top open

The mattress-stitch seam is almost invisible

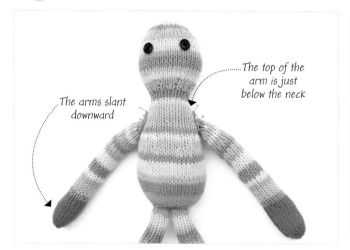

The top of the arm is just below the neck

The arms slant downward

10 Position the arms on either side of the body, just below the neck, and secure them with pins. As you stitch the top of the arm to the body, tuck in the cast-off edge to the inside.

Careful! Be very careful when using pins because they can easily be lost inside the toy, becoming a safety hazard. Count the number of pins before and after use, to be on the safe side.

11 Thread the tail of yarn left before casting on stitches into your needle, then take the needle in and out of the stitches on the cast-on edge. Pull up the tail of yarn tightly to gather these stitches, forming the front of the muzzle. Using the same yarn, join the side edges on the muzzle, using mattress stitch (see p.44). Fasten off the yarn, and do not cut it off but tuck it inside. Add stuffing to fill the muzzle.

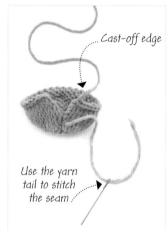

Cast-off edge

Use the yarn tail to stitch the seam

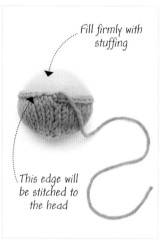

Fill firmly with stuffing

This edge will be stitched to the head

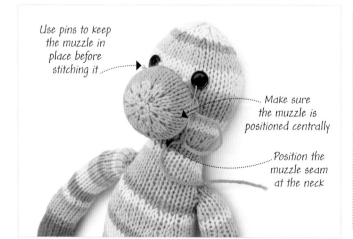

Use pins to keep the muzzle in place before stitching it

Make sure the muzzle is positioned centrally

Position the muzzle seam at the neck

12 Pin the muzzle to the head, just below the button eyes, then stitch it in place, tucking in the cast-off edge to the inside as you do so, and removing the pins one by one.

Tip The muzzle will span about 10 stitches and about 12 rows. To add character to your monkey, slightly compress the muzzle from top to bottom, changing it from a round shape to more of an oval.

13 Sew widely spaced whip stitches along the sides and base of each ear, then gather these stitches to form each ear into a cup shape. Using the same yarn, stitch the ears to the head, one on each side.

Tip The way you position various components, such as the ears, will help give your monkey its own special character, so pin them in place before stitching.

Gather the edges to create a cup shape

Stitch the ears to the side of the head

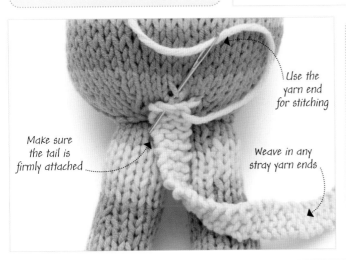

Use the yarn end for stitching

Make sure the tail is firmly attached

Weave in any stray yarn ends

14 Stitch the cast-on edge of the tail to the base of the monkey's body, at the back, then weave in the other yarn end at the cast-off edge of the tail.

Careful! When making knit toys for babies and small children, check that all the components are firmly attached. A thin strip of knitting like this tail might seem pretty harmless, but it might be a choking hazard if it's pulled off.

15 Use a blunt needle and six-stranded embroidery thread to embroider the facial features. Embroider the mouth in backstitch (see p.45) across the center of the muzzle, two straight stitches for nostrils, and another two stitches for eyebrows.

Tip The thread needs to be thick enough not to sink into the knit fabric, so double it up if necessary.

A pair of straight stitches denote nostrils

The mouth is a line of backstitch

How to **Knit Textures**

Plain knit fabrics are smooth and flat, but it is easy to create some surface interest and structure in the form of "bobbles," "clusters," and "popcorns." These raised bumps can be incorporated into fabrics for sweaters and other garments, as well as accessories such as hats and scarves, and housewares such as cushions and throws, either all over or in sections. You will find patterns for a variety of textured stitches on p.120.

Popcorns

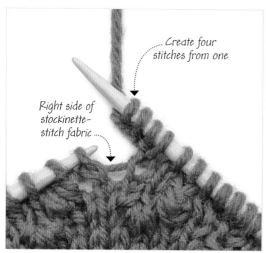

Create four stitches from one

Right side of stockinette-stitch fabric

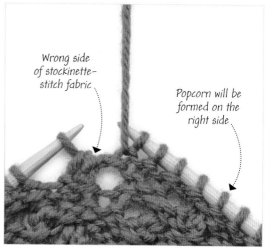

Wrong side of stockinette-stitch fabric

Popcorn will be formed on the right side

1 On the right side, to create a popcorn, insert the right needle knitwise (see p.134) into the next stitch; knit into the front, the back, the front, then the back of the stitch.

2 On the wrong side, when you reach a popcorn, insert the needle tip purlwise (see p.135) into the second stitch; pass it over the first. Repeat for third and fourth stitches.

3 For an all-over popcorn pattern on a background of stockinette stitch, position the popcorns evenly along a row, with an odd number of stitches between each one.

Tip Popcorns and bobbles look most effective on the knit side of a stockinette-stitch fabric, where they really stand out against the smooth background.

Three-into-three stitch

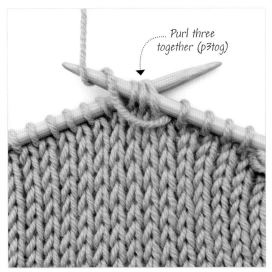

Purl three together (p3tog)

Knit three together

1 On the right side of the fabric, work to the point where the first "bump" should appear. Bring the yarn to the front; insert the needle purlwise (see p.135) through three stitches.

2 Purl the three stitches together, but do not slip them off the needle. Take the yarn to the back and then knit into the back of the three stitches.

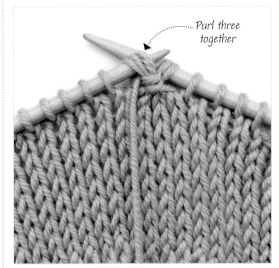

Purl three together

3 Do not slip the stitches off the needle, but bring the yarn to the front again—purl the three stitches together once more, then slip them off the left needle.

4 The three-into-three stitch produces a raised, knotted bobble on the right side of the fabric. Work to the next point and repeat the process to make another bobble.

How to **Knit Simple Twist**

The best way to approach textured knitting is to start simple, then tackle more ambitious techniques as your confidence grows. Here, you can learn the basic principle of twisting and crossing stitches over each other to change the direction of a vertical row. That is the first step to cabling.

Right twist
(Abbreviation = *T2R*)

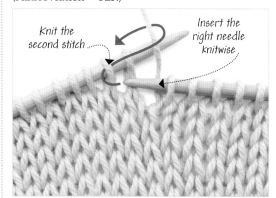

Knit the second stitch

Insert the right needle knitwise

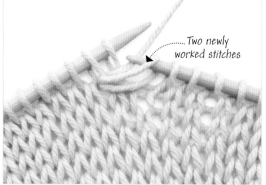

Two newly worked stitches

1 With the yarn at the back of the right needle and in front of the left, knit the second stitch, leaving both the first and second stitches on the left needle.

2 Now knit the first stitch on the left needle and then drop both the old stitches off the needle at the same time.

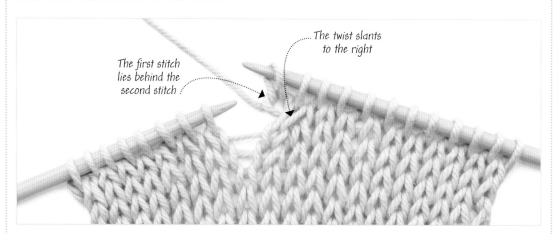

The first stitch lies behind the second stitch

The twist slants to the right

3 Without the use of a cable needle—using just two straight knitting needles and a little ingenuity—this method creates a simple twist: a "one-over-one" two-stitch cable that slants to the right. In a pattern, the instruction will be "T2R."

Left twist
(Abbreviation = *T2L*)

Wrap the yarn around the needle

New stitch

Work behind the first stitch

1 Insert the tip of the right needle behind the first stitch on the left needle and into the second stitch knitwise (see p.134). Wrap the yarn around the left needle.

2 Pull the loop of yarn through the second stitch, behind the first stitch. Be careful not to drop the stitches off the left needle yet.

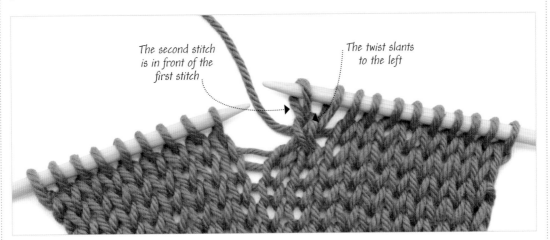

The second stitch is in front of the first stitch

The twist slants to the left

3 Knit the first stitch on the left needle, then drop both old stitches off the left needle. Once again, without having to use a cable needle, this creates a two-stitch cable that slants to the left—a "left twist," which is referred to in a pattern as "T2L."

How to **Knit Cables**

Cables are usually worked in stockinette stitch on a reverse stockinette-stitch (purl) or garter-stitch fabric. Cables are formed by crossing two, three, four, or more stitches over other stitches in the row, using a small, double-ended cable needle to hold stitches while others are being worked. The four-stitch cables shown here are crossed on every sixth row to create a twisted, raised, vertical column.

Cable 4 front

(Abbreviation = C4F)

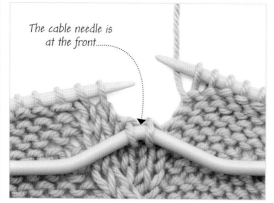

The cable needle is at the front......

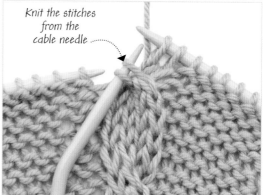

Knit the stitches from the cable needle ......

1 Work to the position of the four stitches which form the cable and slip the first two stitches onto a cable needle. Place the cable needle at the front of the work.

2 Knit the next two stitches on the left needle in the usual way, and then knit the two stitches that are being held on the cable needle.

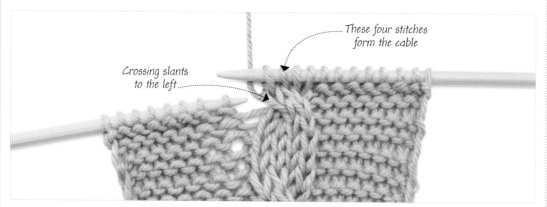

Crossing slants to the left......

...... These four stitches form the cable

3 The first pair of stitches lie on top of the second pair and create a crossing that slants to the left. For this reason, a "front" cable is also known as a "left" cable. The pattern instructions will say "C4F," with the letter C standing for "cable"; the number 4 referring to the number of stitches that form the cable, and the letter F meaning "front."

Cable 4 back

(Abbreviation = *C4B*)

Place the cable needle at the back

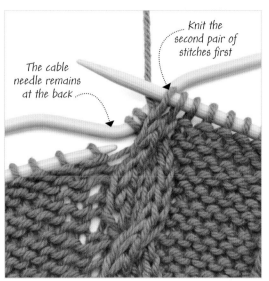

The cable needle remains at the back

Knit the second pair of stitches first

1 Work to the position of the four stitches that form the cable and slip the first two stitches on to a cable needle. Place the cable needle at the back of the work.

2 Knit the next two stitches on the left needle in the usual way, and then knit the two stitches that are being held on the cable needle.

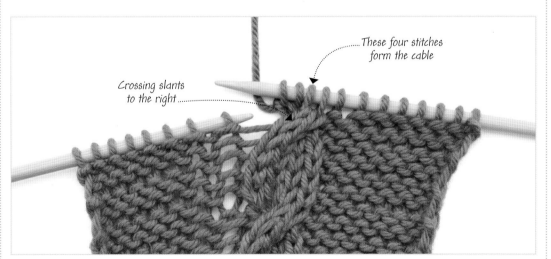

Crossing slants to the right

These four stitches form the cable

3 The first pair of stitches sit behind the second pair and create a crossing that slants to the right. For this reason, a "back" cable is also known as a "right" cable. The pattern instructions will say "C4B" with the letter C standing for "cable"; the number 4 referring to the number of stitches that form the cable, and the letter B denoting "back."

Gallery of **Textured Stitches**

Bobbles, clusters, and puffs add rich texture to knitting and are created using two needles. Cables and twists extend the repertoire of texture—they require additional needles for holding spare stitches.

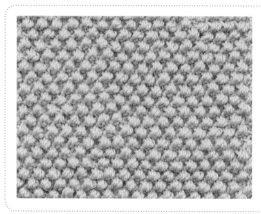

Bobble Stitch

Instructions

Cast on an odd number of sts.
Row 1 (RS): K.
Row 2: K1, *work [p1, k1] twice into next st, pass 2nd, 3rd, and 4th sts over the first st on RH needle, k1, rep from * to end.
Row 3: As row 1.
Row 4: K2, *work [p1, k1] twice into next st, pass 2nd, 3rd, and 4th sts over the first st on RH needle, k1, rep from * to last st, k1.
Rep rows 1–4 to form patt.

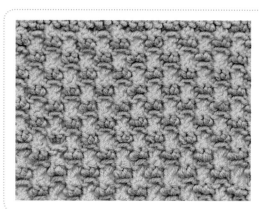

Blackberry Stitch

Instructions

Cast on a multiple of 4sts plus 2 extra sts.
Row 1 (RS): P.
Row 2: K1, *[k1, p1, k1] into next st, p3tog, rep from * to last st, k1.
Row 3: P.
Row 4: K1, *p3tog, [k1, p1, k1] into next st, rep from * to last st, k1.
Rep rows 1–4 to form patt.

Puff Stitch

Instructions

Cast on a multiple of 4sts plus one extra st.
Row 1 (RS): K.
Row 2: P.
Row 3: K1, *p3tog without removing these sts from needle, yo, reinsert RH needle into 3 previously worked sts and p3tog, this time removing them from LH needle, k1, rep from * to end.
Row 4: P.
Rep rows 1–4 to form patt.

Cable-effect Stitch

Instructions

Cast on a multiple of 5sts plus 2 extra sts.
Note: The stitch count varies from row to row.
Row 1 (RS): P2, *yarn to back of work between 2 needles, s1 purlwise, k2, pass slipped st over last 2 k sts and off RH needle, p2, rep from * to end.
Row 2: K2, *p1, yo, p1, k2, rep from * to end.
Row 3: P2, *k3, p2, rep from * to end.
Row 4: K2, *p3, k2, rep from * to end.
Rep rows 1–4 to form patt.

Four-stitch Cable Pattern

Instructions
Special abbreviations

C4F: Slip next 2sts on to cable needle and hold at front of work, k2 from LH needle, then k2 from cable needle.
C4B: Slip next 2sts on to cable needle and hold at back of work, k2 from LH needle, then k2 from cable needle.

Cast on a multiple of 14sts plus 3 extra sts.
Row 1 (RS): P3, *k4, p3, rep from * to end.
Row 2: K3, *p4, k3, rep from * to end.
Row 3: P3, *k4, p3, C4F, p3, rep from *.
Row 4: Rep row 2.
Row 5: P3, *C4B, p3, k4, p3, rep from * to end.
Rep rows 2–5 to form patt.

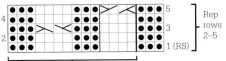

Rep = 14sts

Six-stitch Cable Pattern

Instructions
Special abbreviations

C6F: Slip next 3sts on to cable needle and hold at front of work, k3 from LH needle, then k3 from cable needle.
C6B: Slip next 3sts on to cable needle and hold at back of work, k3 from LH needle, then k3 from cable needle.

Cast on a multiple of 18sts plus 3 extra sts.
Row 1 (RS): P3, *k6, p3, rep from * to end.
Row 2 and all even-numbered (WS) rows: K3, *p6, k3, rep from * to end.
Row 3: P3, *k6, p3, C6F, p3, rep from * to end.
Row 5: Rep row 1.
Row 7: P3, *C6B, p3, k6, p3, rep from * to end.
Row 9: Rep row 1.
Rep rows 2–9 to form patt.

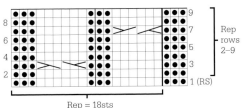

Rep = 18sts

Medallion Cable Stitch

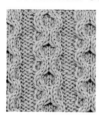

Instructions
Special abbreviations

C4F: Slip next 2sts on to cable needle and hold at front of work, k2 from LH needle, then k2 from cable needle.
C4B: Slip next 2sts on to cable needle and hold at back of work, wk2 from LH needle, then k2 from cable needle.

Cast on a multiple of 22sts plus 3 extra sts.
Row 1 (RS): P3, *k8, p3, rep from *.
Row 2 and all foll even-numbered (WS) rows: K3, *p8, k3, rep from * to end.

Row 3: P3, *k8, p3, C4B, C4F, p3, rep from * to end.
Row 5: P3, *C4B, C4F, p3, k8, p3, rep from * to end.
Row 7: P3, *k8, p3, C4F, C4B, p3, rep from * to end.
Row 9: P3, *C4F, C4B, p3, k8, p3, rep from * to end.
Rep rows 2–9 to form patt.

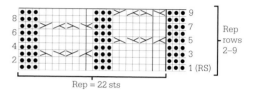

Rep = 22 sts

Rep rows 2–9

Cable Boxes

Instructions
Special abbreviations

C4F: Slip next 2sts on to cable needle and hold at front of work, k2 from LH needle, then k2 from cable needle.

Cast on a multiple of 8sts plus 4 extra sts.
Row 1 (RS): *P4, k4, rep from * to last 4sts, p4.
Row 2: *K4, p4, k4, rep from * to last 4sts, p4.
Row 3: As row 1.
Row 4: As row 2.
Row 5: *P4, C4F, rep from * to last 4sts, p4.
Rows 6 and 7: As row 2.
Row 8: As row 1.
Row 9: As row 2.
Row 10: As row 1.
Row 11: *C4F, p4, rep from* to last 4sts, C4F.
Row 12: As row 1.
Rep rows 1–12 to form patt.

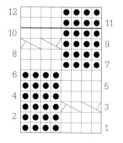

Garter Zigzag Twist

Instructions
Special abbreviations

T2R (twist 2 right): Skip first st on LH needle and k 2nd st through front of loop (do not drop st off LH needle), then k first st on LH needle and drop both sts off LH needle at same time.
T2L (twist 2 left): Skip first st on LH needle and k 2nd st by taking RH needle behind first st to do so (do not drop st off LH needle), then k first st on LH needle and drop both sts off LH needle at same time.

Row 1 (RS): K.
Row 2: *K5, p1, rep from * to last st, k1.
Row 3: K1, *T2L, k4, rep from * to end.
Row 4: K4, p1, *k5, p1, rep from * to last 2sts, k2.
Row 5: K2, T2L, *k4, T2L, rep from * to last 3sts, k3.
Row 6: K3, p1, *k5, p1, rep from * to last 3sts, k3.
Row 7: K3, T2L, *k4, T2L, rep from * to last 2sts, k2.
Row 8: K2, p1, *k5, p1, rep from * to last 4sts, k4.
Row 9: *K4, T2L, rep from * to last st, k1.
Row 10: K1, *p1, k5, rep from * to end.
Row 11: *K4, T2R, rep from * to last st, k1.
Row 12: Rep row 8.
Row 13: K3, T2R, *k4, T2R, rep from * to last 2sts, k2.
Row 14: Rep row 6.
Row 15: K2, T2R, *k4, T2R, rep from * to last 3sts, k3.
Row 16: Rep row 4.
Row 17: K1, *T2R, k4, rep from * to end.
Row 18: Rep row 2.
Rep rows 3–18 to form patt.

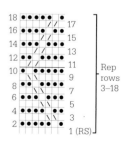

Rep rows 3–18

Fan Cable

Instructions
Special abbreviations

CR2R: Skip first st on LH needle and k 2nd st through front of loop (do not drop st off LH needle), then p first st on LH needle and drop both sts off this needle at same time.

CR2L: Skip first st on LH needle and p 2nd st by taking RH needle behind first st to do so (so do not drop st off LH needle), then k first st on LH needle and drop both sts off together.

Cast on a multiple of 14sts plus 2 extra sts.
Row 1 and all foll alt rows (WS): P.
Row 2: *K6, CR2R, k6, rep from * to last 2sts, k2.
Row 4: *K5, CR2R, p1, k6, rep from * to last 2sts, k2.
Row 6: *K4, CR2R, p2, k6, rep from * to last 2sts, k2.
Row 8: *K3, CR2R, p3, k6, rep from * to last 2sts, k2.
Row 10: *K2, CR2R, p4, k6, rep from * to last 2sts, k2.
Row 12: *K8, CR2L, k4, rep from * to last 2sts, k2.
Row 14: *K8, p1, CR2L, k3, rep from * to last 2sts, k2.
Row 16: *K8, p2, CR2L, K2, rep from * to last 2sts, k2.
Row 18: *K8, p3, CR2L, k1, rep from * to last 2sts, k2.
Row 20: *K8, p4, CR2L, rep from * to last 2sts, k2.
Rep rows 1–12 to form patt.

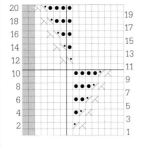

Diamond Cable

Instructions
Special abbreviations

CR4L: Place 2sts on cable needle and leave at front of work, p2, then k2 from cable needle.
CR4R: Place 2sts on cable needle and leave at back of work, k2, then p2 from cable needle.
C4F: Place 2sts on cable needle and leave at front of work, k2, then k2 from cable needle.

Cast on a multiple of 20sts.
Row 1: *P8, C4F, p8, rep from * to end.
Row 2: *K8, p4, k8, rep from * to end.
Row 3: *P6, CR4R, CR4L, p6, rep from * to end.
Row 4: *K6, p2, k4, p2, k6, rep from * to end.
Row 5: *P4, CR4R, p4, CR4L, p4, rep from * to end.
Row 6: *K4, p2, k8, p2, k4, rep from * to end.
Row 7: *P2, CR4R, p8, CR4L, p2, rep from * to end.
Row 8: *K2, p2, k12, p2, k2, rep from * to end.
Row 9: *P2, CR4L, p8, CR4R, p2, rep from * to end.
Row 10: As row 6.
Row 11: *P4, CR4L, p4, CR4R, p4, rep from * to end.
Row 12: As row 6.
Row 13: *P6, CR4L, CR4R, p6, rep from * to end.
Row 14: As row 2.
Rep rows 1–14 to form patt.

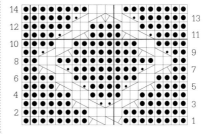

Smocking

Instructions
Special abbreviation

Smock 5sts: Slip next 5 sts onto cable needle and leave at front of work, bring yarn to the front of work, and wrap counterclockwise around these stitches twice so that yarn now sits at back of work. Work (K1, p3, k1) from cable needle.

Cast on a multiple of 8sts, plus 7 extra sts.
Row 1 (RS): P1, k1, *p3, k1, rep from * to last st, p1.
Row 2: K1, p1, *k3, p1, rep from * to last st, k1.
Row 3: P1, smock 5sts, *p3, smock 5sts, rep from * to last st, p1.
Row 4: As row 2.
Row 5: As row 1. Rep last 2 rows once more, and row 2 again.
Row 9: P1, k1, p3, *smock 5sts, p3, rep from * to last 2sts, k1, p1.
Rows 10 and 12: As row 2.
Row 11: As row 1. Rep rows 1–12 to form patt.

Garter Stitch Cable

Instructions
Special abbreviation

C8F: Place 4sts on cable needle and leave at front of work, k4, then k4 from cable needle.

Cast on a multiple of 18sts.
Row 1 (RS): *P5, k8, p5, rep from * to end.
Row 2: *K9, p4, k5, rep from * to end.
Rep last 2 rows twice more.
Row 7: P5, *C8F, p5, rep from * to end.
Row 8: *K5, p4, k9, rep from * to end.
Row 9: As row 1.
Rep last 2 rows four times more, then row 8 again.
Row 19: As row 7.
Row 20: As row 2.
Row 21: As row 1.
Row 22: As row 2.
Row 23: As row 1.
Row 24: As row 2.
Rep rows 1–24 to form patt.

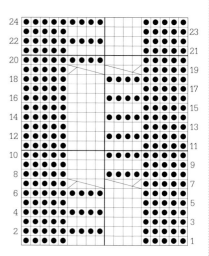

Wavy Cable

Instructions
Special abbreviations

CR2R: Skip first st on LH needle and k 2nd st through front of loop (do not drop st off LH needle), then p first st on LH needle and drop both sts off this needle at same time.
CR2L: Skip first st on LH needle and p 2nd st by taking RH needle behind first st to do so (so do not drop st off LH needle), then k first st on LH needle and drop both sts off together.

Cast on a multiple of 3sts (a minimum of 9sts).
Row 1 (RS): *P1, CR2R, rep from * to end.
Row 2: *K1, p1, k1, rep from * to end.
Row 3: *CR2R, p1, rep from * to end.
Row 4: *K2, p1, rep from * to end.
Row 5: *K1, p2, rep from * to end.
Row 6: As row 4.
Row 7: *CR2L, p1, rep from * to end.
Row 8: As row 2.

Row 9: *P1, CR2L, rep from * to end.
Row 10: *P1, k2, rep from * to end.
Row 11: *P2, k1, rep from * to end.
Row 12: As row 10.
Rep rows 1–12 to form patt.

Horseshoe Cable

Instructions
Special abbreviations

C4F: Slip next 2sts on to cable needle and hold at front of work, k2 from LH needle, then k2 from cable needle.

C4B: Slip next 2sts on to cable needle and hold at back of work, k2 from LH needle, then k2 from cable needle.

Cast on a multiple of 22sts plus 3 extra sts.
Row 1 (RS): P3, *k8, p3, rep from * to end.
Row 2 and all even-numbered (WS) rows: K3, *p8, k3, rep from * to end.

Row 3: P3, *k8, p3, C4B, C4F, p3, rep from * to end.
Row 5: As row 1.
Row 7: P3, *C4B, C4F, p3, k8, p3, rep from * to end.
Row 9: Rep row 1.
Rep rows 2–9 to form patt.

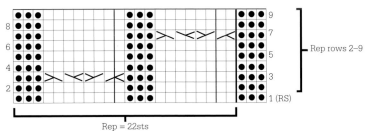

Rep rows 2–9

Rep = 22sts

Woven Cable

Instructions
Special abbreviations

C6F: Place 3sts on cable needle and leave at front of work, k3, then k3 from cable needle.

C6B: Place 3sts on cable needle and leave at back of work, k3, then k3 from cable needle.

Cast on a multiple of 6sts (a minimum of 12sts).
Row 1 (RS): K.

Row 2 and all foll alt rows: P.
Row 3: K3, *C6B, rep from * to last 3sts, k3.
Row 5: K.
Row 7: *C6F, rep from * to end.
Row 8: As row 2.
Rep rows 1–8 to form patt.

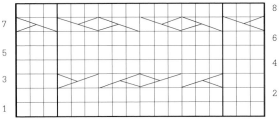

How to **Attach a Fastener**

While buttons are the traditional fastener for most knit garments, zippers also have their place. The stiffness of a zipper is not always compatible with the softness and stretchiness of a knit fabric, so you must always choose your with care. For example, a zipper might be the best choice for a jacket made from a firm knit fabric, or for a bag or a cushion cover.

Sewing in zipper

1 A zipper is often inserted between two side edges of a knit fabric, so for a good finish make sure the selvedges are as neat as possible. The knit edges will usually cover the fabric edges of the zipper, unless you want to make a feature of the zipper.

Close the zipper before pinning

Remember Match the zipper's color and weight to the yarn used for knitting and the function of the knit item. For example, a chunky zipper looks out of place on a lightweight knit fabric.

2 With right sides facing, pin the top and bottom of the knit fabric to the closed zipper. Position the edge of the knitting over the teeth.

Pin the center of the fabric to the center of the zipper, then work outward from this point, easing the rows to distribute them evenly.

Use contrast-colored thread for basting

Make sure the zipper teeth are covered by the edge of the knit fabric

3 Baste the zipper in place. Then take a sharp, large-eyed sewing needle and either yarn or sewing thread in a color that matches your knit fabric. Sew the zipper to the knit fabric, using backstitch (see p.45), following the same vertical line of knit stitches.

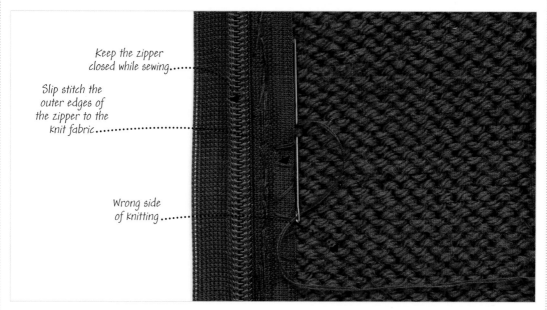

Keep the zipper closed while sewing

Slip stitch the outer edges of the zipper to the knit fabric

Wrong side of knitting

4 Turn the work inside out and, using matching sewing thread, whip stitch the fabric edge of the zipper to the knit fabric, or use a hemming stitch, sewing into the backs of the same vertical line of stitches. Repeat for the other edge of the zipper.

Make a Cabled Cushion

This attractive cushion cover, made in a soft, pure-wool yarn, will help you to practice knitting cables. Aran-weight yarn is the traditional choice for cable knits and produces quicker results than double knitting.

Instructions

Difficulty level
Moderate

Size
16 x 16 in (40 x 40 cm) approx.

Yarn
Rowan Pure Wool Aran 100 g
689 Burlesque x 3

Needles
1 pair of US8 (5 mm/UK6) needles
Cable needle

Notions
14 in or 16 in (35 cm or 40 cm) zipper
Blunt tapestry needle

Gauge
18 sts and 21 rows to 4 in (10 cm) over patt
using US8 (5 mm/UK6) needles

Special abbreviations
(See also pp.118–119.)

C8F
S4 to cable needle, hold in front,
k4, k4 from cable needle.

C4B
RS: S4 to cable needle, hold in back,
k4, k4 from cable needle.

**689
Burlesque x 3**

1 pair of US8 (5 mm/UK6) needles

Cable needle

Pattern
Work all RS (odd) rows on chart from R to L
and all WS (even) rows from L to R.

Cushion Side (make 2)
Cast on 66sts using cable cast-on method
(see p.36).
Row 1 (RS): K11, [inc in next st, k4, inc in
next st, k15] twice, inc in next st, k4, inc in
next st, k to end. (72sts)
Row 2 (WS): K9, [p12, k9] to end.

Commence patt
Row 1 (RS): K9, [work next 21sts as in
chart] three times.

CHART

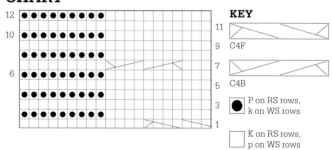

Row 2 (WS): [Work next 21sts as in chart]
three times, k9.
Cont working last 2 rows in patt as set,
repeating 12 rows of chart until work
measures 40cm (16in), ending with a RS
row.
Dec row: K9, (p3, p2tog, p2, p2tog, p3, k9)
three times. (66sts)
Cast off.

129

Backstitch seam

If it is worked on the wrong side, a backstitch seam forms a ridge on the wrong side but, if worked well, has a neat finish on the outside. In this case, make sure the two halves of the cable pattern match up.

Garter stitch creates a lightly textured background .....

Garter stitch

The garter stitch gives a light texture to the background, so that it forms a contrast to the intertwining ropes of cable stitches. The whole thing makes a very attractive fabric that feels sensuous to the touch.

Zipper

The cast-on edges form a very neat, ropelike border to accommodate the zipper. A zipper allows the cushion pad to be removed so that the knit cover can be cleaned.

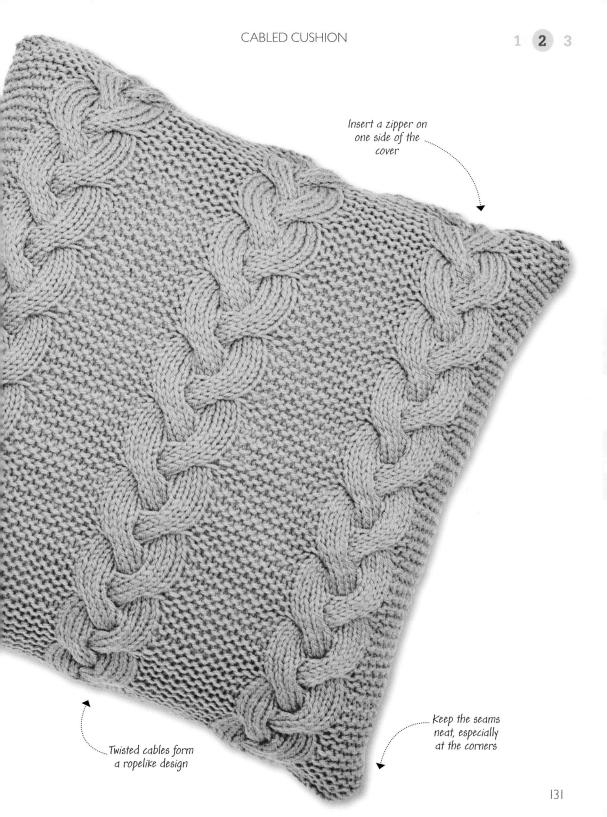

Insert a zipper on
one side of the
cover

Twisted cables form
a ropelike design

Keep the seams
neat, especially
at the corners

3

Take It Further

If you have been practicing all the techniques from the previous chapters, you have now built up quite a skills base—and with it, no doubt, a stash of scrap yarn. Get ready to use that yarn to knit up some colorwork swatches and lace. Then you can tackle other techniques and projects, like the ones shown in this chapter, with confidence.

Learn to knit:

Raglan Sweater
pp.142–147

Baby's Cardigan
pp.150–153

Mittens
pp.154–157

Fair Isle Arm Warmers
pp.166–169

Peekaboo Lace Scarf
pp.180–183

How to **Slip Stitches Knitwise**

In addition to knitting or purling stitches, sometimes you will need to slip stitches. This means moving one or more stitches from one needle to another—or onto a cable needle or stitch holder—to keep them in reserve for a while. Follow pattern instructions, slipping stitches knitwise only when instructed to do so, since this twists the stitch.

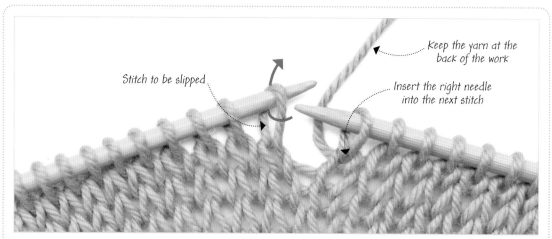

Stitch to be slipped

Keep the yarn at the back of the work

Insert the right needle into the next stitch

1 When a pattern instructs you to slip a stitch knitwise, insert the tip of the right needle into the next stitch on the left needle, from left to right, through the front of the loop, as if you were going to work a knit stitch (see p.40). Keep the yarn at the back of the work as you do this.

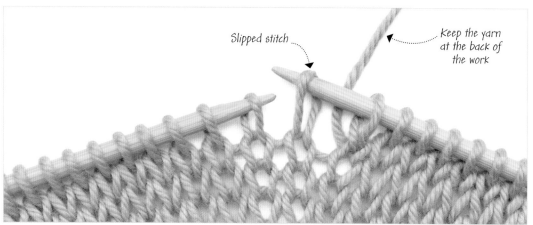

Slipped stitch

Keep the yarn at the back of the work

2 Do not work the stitch: just slip it from the left needle on to the right needle. The slipped stitch now sits on the right needle, with the left side of the loop at the front of the needle, facing the opposite way of the worked stitches next to it.

How to **Slip Stitches Purlwise**

Unless you are instructed to do otherwise, you will usually be expected to slip stitches purlwise, as if you were beginning to work a purl stitch. This is the method you will use when slipping stitches onto a stitch holder, to be worked on later, for example, because this method ensures that the stitches are not twisted.

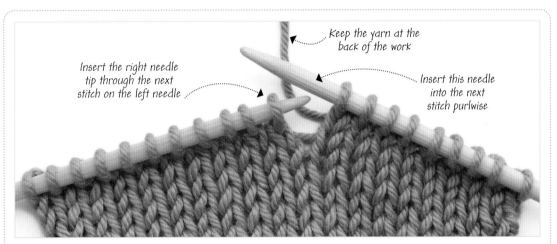

Insert the right needle tip through the next stitch on the left needle

Keep the yarn at the back of the work

Insert this needle into the next stitch purlwise

1 When a pattern simply instructs you to slip one or more stitches, without specifying how you should do this, you should assume that it means that the stitches are to be slipped purlwise. To do this, insert the tip of the right needle, from right to left, through the front loop of the next stitch on the left needle.

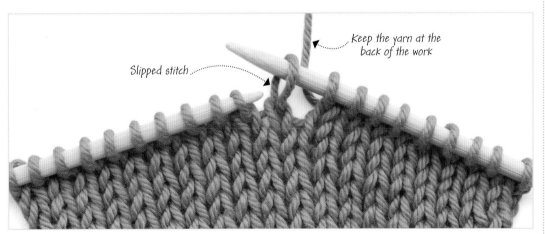

Slipped stitch

Keep the yarn at the back of the work

2 You will have inserted the right needle as if you were about to work a purl stitch, but, instead, you slip the stitch on to the right needle. The slipped stitch now sits on the right needle with the right side of the loop at the front, like the worked stitches next to it.

How to **Knit Through Back Loop**

Sometimes a knitting pattern will instruct you to knit—or purl—a stitch through the back loop. The abbreviation for knitting one stitch in this way is "k1 tbl." The method for doing this is illustrated below—and the same principle applies for knitting two stitches through the back loop (k2 tbl) and for purling through the back loop (p1 tbl or p2 tbl).

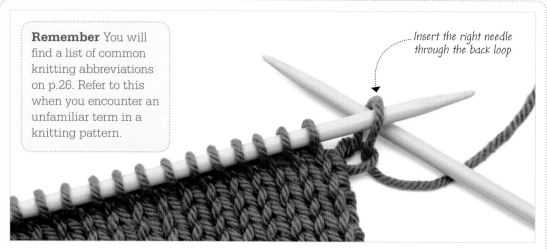

> **Remember** You will find a list of common knitting abbreviations on p.26. Refer to this when you encounter an unfamiliar term in a knitting pattern.

... Insert the right needle through the back loop

1 When you are instructed to "k1 tbl" (knit one stitch through the back loop), insert the tip of the right needle from right to left through the next stitch on the left needle, and through the part of the stitch loop that sits behind the needle.

... Slip the completed stitch from the left to the right needle

The stitch is twisted

2 Wrap the yarn around the tip of the right needle and complete the knit stitch in the usual way. Knitting through the back loop twists the stitch in the row below, so that the legs of the stitch cross at the base.

How to **Knit Smooth Diagonal Cast off**

This technique is often used on a shoulder edge, to help create a neat seam. The example illustrated below assumes that you are working a pattern where the shoulder edge is cast off in groups of five stitches. If you were to cast off five stitches on every other row, you would create a stepped edge—but this method helps to smooth out the bumps.

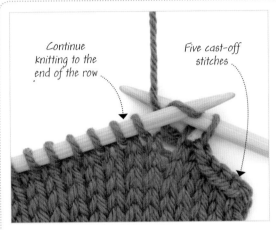

Continue knitting to the end of the row

Five cast-off stitches

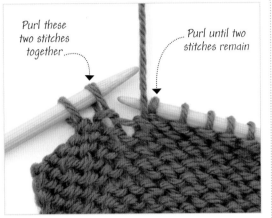

Purl these two stitches together

Purl until two stitches remain

1 Cast off five stitches using the casting off knitwise method described on p.42, leaving the last stitch of the cast off on the right needle.

2 Continue knitting to the end of the row, turn and purl until there are only two stitches remaining on the left needle; purl these two stitches together.

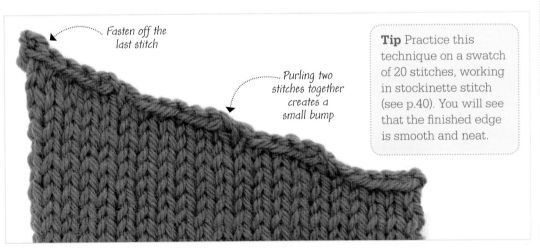

Fasten off the last stitch

Purling two stitches together creates a small bump

Tip Practice this technique on a swatch of 20 stitches, working in stockinette stitch (see p.40). You will see that the finished edge is smooth and neat.

3 Turn the work, so that the right side (knit side) is facing you, then repeat steps 1 and 2 as many times as necessary, until you have only one stitch remaining. Then fasten off this stitch (as described on p.53).

How to **Knit Neat Edges**

A piece of knit fabric typically has four edges: the cast-on and cast-off edges and the two side edges, which are called selvedges.
Neat edges look more professional and are easier to sew up. Here are two simple methods of creating neat selvedges.

Garter selvedge

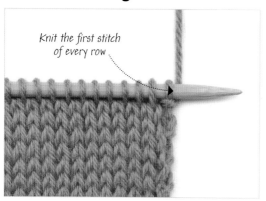

Knit the first stitch of every row

Each bump equals two rows

1 This method is good for edges that will not be sewn up, on items such as scarves and blankets. On every row, whether it is a knit or purl row, knit the first and last stitches.

2 On a stockinette-stitch fabric, the garter selvedge technique will encourage the fabric to lie flat; it also creates a series of small bumps or "pits" down the edge.

Slipped garter selvedge

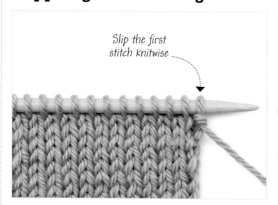

Slip the first stitch knitwise

Little bumps along the edge can make picking up stitches much easier

1 At the beginning of every row, slip the first stitch "knitwise," by inserting the right needle into the front of the stitch from left to right, as if you were going to knit it.

2 On every row, whether it is a knit or purl row, knit the last stitch. This method produces an edge that is firmer than the garter selvedge shown above.

How to **Pick Up Stitches**

Picking up stitches along the edge of a piece of knitting—typically, to create a neckband or armhole border—is something even experienced knitters find challenging. Practice on knit swatches to perfect the techniques before tackling a knit garment.

Cast on/off edge

With RS facing, insert the right needle into the first stitch, wrap the yarn around and pull the loop through; repeat in each stitch.

With a crochet hook

1 Insert the hook into the first stitch, wrap the yarn around the hook from left to right and pull the loop through to the front.

2 Transfer the loop from the hook onto a knitting needle, pulling the yarn to tighten it; repeat with each stitch along the row.

Along row ends

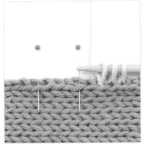

1 Use pins to mark the row ends along the selvedge, evenly spacing the pins at the end of every four rows, as shown here.

2 Pick up and knit three stitches between each pair of pins, inserting the needle into the center of the edge stitch.

Along a curved edge

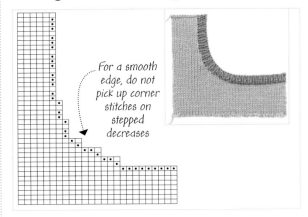

For a smooth edge, do not pick up corner stitches on stepped decreases

On most armhole borders and neckbands you will need to pick up stitches along a curved edge. As a general rule, pick up one stitch in each cast-off stitch and three stitches for every four rows ends.

How to **Measure Gauge**

You should always knit a swatch before starting work on a project, to make sure that you can achieve the stitch size (gauge) stated in the pattern, otherwise your finished item could be too large or too small. Use the same yarn and needles required for the pattern and create a gauge swatch about 5 in (13 cm) square to make measuring easy.

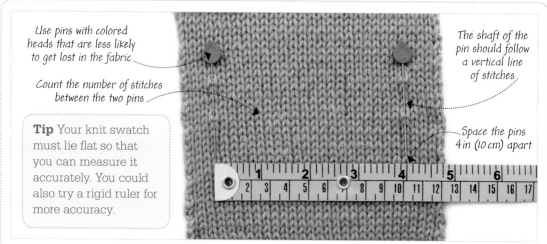

Use pins with colored heads that are less likely to get lost in the fabric

The shaft of the pin should follow a vertical line of stitches

Count the number of stitches between the two pins

Space the pins 4 in (10 cm) apart

Tip Your knit swatch must lie flat so that you can measure it accurately. You could also try a rigid ruler for more accuracy.

1 Cast on more stitches than the number stated in the gauge guide—so, if there are 22sts to 4 in (10 cm) in your pattern, cast on 28–30 stitches. Knit until the work measures 5 in (13 cm), then place two pins, 4 in (10 cm) apart, and count the stitches in between.

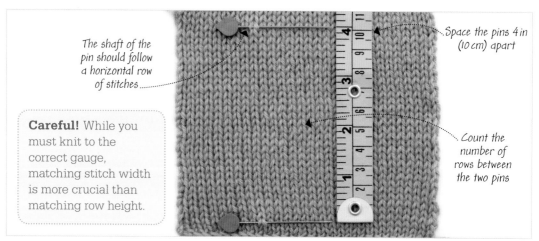

The shaft of the pin should follow a horizontal row of stitches

Space the pins 4 in (10 cm) apart

Careful! While you must knit to the correct gauge, matching stitch width is more crucial than matching row height.

Count the number of rows between the two pins

2 Count the number of rows to 4 in (10 cm) in a similar way. If you have fewer stitches and rows than the number stated in the pattern, make another swatch using smaller needles; if you have more, use larger needles. Continue until you achieve the right gauge.

How to **Block Knits**

Most knitting projects involving pieces to be joined together will benefit from blocking—a process of stretching and shaping knit fabric to achieve the correct shape and dimensions. Blocking also makes the surface of the knitting look more even. Check your pattern instructions and the ball band of your yarn before choosing which method to use.

Wet blocking

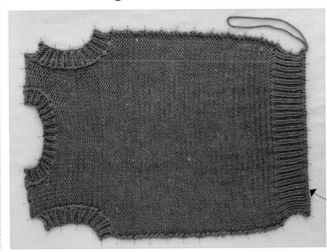

Wet blocking is the best method of shaping your knitting. Immerse the piece in lukewarm water, then gently squeeze out most of the moisture, or use a spray bottle to dampen the knitting. Place it on layers of towels, pin out into shape, and let it dry.

Avoid blocking ribbed bands because it can make them less stretchy

Steam blocking

Steam block your knitting only if this is the method recommended. Pin out the knitting on an ironing board or on layers of towels, place a clean damp cloth on top, and use an iron to create steam, barely touching the cloth. Let it dry before removing the pins.

Do not press too hard or let the iron come into contact with the knitting

Knit a Raglan Sweater

This classic style, knit in a chunky yarn to suit a man or woman, features raglan shaping—a useful technique to master, because it creates a well-fitting garment that is flattering and comfortable to wear.

Instructions

Difficulty Level
Moderate

Size
Adult unisex, to fit chest
38 (42, 46) in, [96.5 (107, 117) cm]

Yarn
Cascade 128 Superwash Chunky
(100 g) 893 Ruby x 8 (9, 10)

Needles
1 pair of US10 (6 mm/ UK4)
needles
1 pair of US10½ (6.5 mm/UK3)
needles
4 stitch holders

Notions
Blunt tapestry needle

Gauge
15 sts and 20 rows to 4 in (10 cm)
over st st on US10½ (6.5 mm/UK3)
needles

893
Ruby x 8, (9, 10)

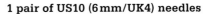

1 pair of US10 (6 mm/UK4) needles

1 pair of US10½ (6.5 mm/UK3) needles

Pattern

Back
Using US10 (6 mm/ UK4) needles,
cast on 76 (84, 90) sts using knit-on
cast-on method (see p.34).

Ribbing
Row 1: K1 (1, 0) * k2, p2 * last 3
(3, 2) stitches, k3 (3, 2).
Row 2: P3 (3, 2) * k2, p2 * last
st, p1 (1,0).
Rep these two rows five times
more, or until work measures 3 in
(7 cm), ending with a WS row.
Change to US10½ (6.5 mm/UK3)
needles and beg with a k row
continue in st st until the work
measures 17½ (18¼, 19) in [44 (46,
48) cm] from the cast
on edge, ending with a WS row.

Raglan Armhole Shaping
With RS facing, cast off 3 sts at beg
of next two rows. [70 (78, 84) sts]

Dec 1 st at each end of next four
rows. [62 (70, 76) sts]
Next row (RS): K2, skpo, k to
last 4 sts, k2tog, k2.
Next row: P.
Rep last two rows, then dec as
set on each RS row until 22 (24,
26) sts rem. Make sure the last p
row is worked.
Slip rem sts onto a stitch holder
(see p.134).

Front
Work the same as the back until
there are 36 sts left after the start
of the raglan armhole shaping,
ending with a p row.

Left Front Raglan and Neck Shaping
Next row (RS): K2, skpo, k10,
slip rem 22 sts from the left
needle on to a stitch holder.

Turn the knitting so WS is
facing and working only on
the 13 sts rem.
Next row (WS): P2tog, p to end.
(12 sts)
Next row (RS): K2, skpo, k to last
2 sts, k2tog.
Next row (WS): P.
Rep these two rows three times.
(4 sts)
Next row (RS): K2, skpo. (3 sts)
Next row (WS): Ptog, p1. (2 sts)
Next row (RS): K2tog. (1st)
Cut yarn, leaving a tail at least 8 in
(20 cm) long, and fasten off.

Right Front Raglan and Neck Shaping
Leaving the central 8 sts on the
holder, slip the 14 sts for the right
side of the neck back onto a needle.
Rejoin yarn at center, k to the last
4 sts, k2tog, k2. (13 sts)

Next row (WS): P11, p2tog. (12sts)

Next row (RS): K2tog, k to last 4sts, k2tog, k2. (10sts)

Next row: P.

Next row: K2tog, k to last 4sts, k2tog, k2. (8sts)

Next row: P.

Next row: K2tog, k to last 4sts, k2tog, k2. (6sts)

Next row: P.

Next row: K2tog twice, k2. (4sts)

Next row: P.

Next row: K2tog, k2. (3sts)

Next row: P1, p2tog. (2sts)

Next row: K2tog. (1st)

Cut yarn and fasten off.

Sleeves

Work two the same.

Cast on 32 (36, 40)sts using US10 (6mm/UK4) needles and knit-on cast on.

Ribbing

Row 1 (RS): K1, *k2, p2, rep from * to last 3sts, k3.

Row 2 (WS): P3, *k2, p2, rep from * to last st, p1.

Rep these two rows five more times.

Change to US10½ (6.5mm/UK3) needles and cont in st st with the first row as follows:

Next row (INC) (RS): Kfb, k7 (8,9), kfb, k7 (8,9), kfb, k7 (8,9), kfb, k7 (8,9), kfb.37 (41, 45)sts

Next row (WS): P.

Next row: K.

Next row: P.

Next row (INC) (RS): Kfb, k to last 2sts, kfb, k1. Work five rows in st st, ending with a WS row. Rep these six rows, inc as described until there are 63 (67, 71)sts.

All incs should be worked on RS rows.

Once there are 63 (67, 71)sts cont in st st until the sleeve measures 18 (19, 20)in [46 (48, 50)cm] from the cast on edge, ending with a WS row.

Shape top of raglan sleeves

Cast off 3sts at the beg of the next two rows 56 (61, 65)sts

Decrease (using k2tog/p2tog) 1st at each end of the next four rows. 48 (53, 57)sts

Next row (RS): K2, sl1, k1, psso, k to last 4sts, k2tog, k2. 46 (51, 55)sts

Next row (WS): P.

Rep these two rows, dec on every RS row until 9sts remain.

Slip rem 9sts onto a stitch holder.

Join the pieces together

Sew both sleeves to the front, and the right sleeve to the back, leaving the seam between the back and the left sleeve open. (The right and left is determined as it would be worn.) Use mattress stitch to join the seams.

Neckband

Using US10 (6mm/UK4) needles and with the RS of the sweater facing, rejoin yarn and knit across the 9sts from the stitch holder at the top of the left sleeve.

Next, pick up and knit 8sts down the left side of the front of the neck. Knit 8sts from the front stitch holder.

Pick up and knit 8sts up the right side of the front neck.

Knit 9sts from the stitch holder at the top of the right shoulder.

Knit 22 (24, 26)sts from the back stitch holder. 64 (66, 68)sts

Next row (WS): P2, kfb p2 *k2, p2* to last 3sts, inc in next st, p2. 66 (70, 72)sts

Work four rows in k2, p2 rib as set by this last row.

Next row (RS): Cast off in rib patt, making sure the cast off is not tight. It must be stretchy enough for the sweater to fit over the wearer's head.

Join the pieces together

Sew the edges of the neckband together using mattress stitch. Sew left raglan seam in place. Sew side seams and sleeve seams together using mattress stitch.

1 The lower ribbed edge of the sweater is in double rib: k2, p2. There are extra stitches at the beginning and end of each row to allow for a small amount of each edge to be hidden within the side seams.

Careful! Try to make sure that your cast-on edge is not too tight, since the point of including a ribbed band is to create a slightly stretchy edge that fits well.

Ribbing is created by working k2, p2

Leave a yarn tail for sewing side seams

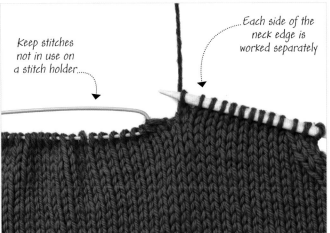

Keep stitches not in use on a stitch holder

Each side of the neck edge is worked separately

2 The decreases in the pattern create an attractive sloping ridge characteristic of raglan shaping. When you reach the top of the armhole shaping, you will also need to shape the neck, and this requires you to transfer some stitches on to a holder for later use.

Tip If you don't have enough stitch holders, try improvising with a length of cotton yarn.

3 In this view of the wrong side of the sweater front, you can clearly see how the stitches for the center part of the neck are being kept on a holder and the neck shaping is being worked on a small number of stitches.

Careful! Follow the instructions carefully, because it is easy to lose track when working a series of decreases. Use a sticky note to mark your place in the pattern.

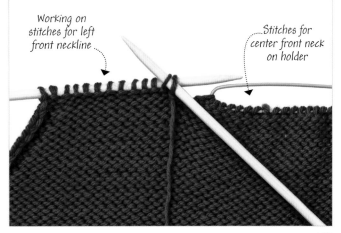

Working on stitches for left front neckline

Stitches for center front neck on holder

4 Once the left side has been completed, you will be required to keep the stitches for the center of the neck on the holder, and work the right side.

Why? The instructions for this sweater tell you, row by row, how to work each side of the neck. Some patterns, however, tell you to "work right side to match, reversing shapings," leaving you to figure it out for yourself.

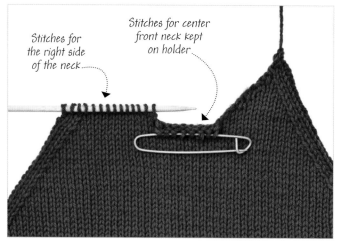

Stitches for the right side of the neck

Stitches for center front neck kept on holder

5 Once you have made the back, front, and both sleeves, you will need to sew together the raglan seams on the front and the right-hand seam on the back, using mattress stitch, leaving the seam between the back and the left sleeve open for the time being. After sewing the seams, weave in the remaining yarn tails, taking them back along the seams on the inside. Leave all the spare stitches on their holders.

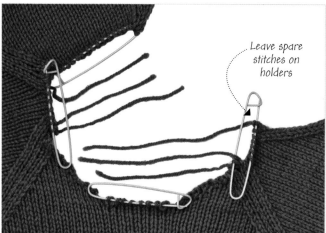

Leave spare stitches on holders

6 To make the neckband, with the right side of the sweater facing you and starting with the stitch holder at the top of the left sleeve, knit these stitches, then pick up and knit eight stitches down the left side of the front neck. Knit the stitches from the next stitch holder.

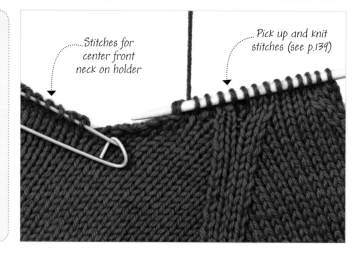

Stitches for center front neck on holder

Pick up and knit stitches (see p.139)

7 Continue by picking up and knitting another eight stitches up the other side of the front neck, then knit the stitches from the remaining two stitch holders.

Tip Instead of using straight needles, you may find it easier to use a circular needle, because it is more flexible. Circular needles are designed for working in rounds; in this case you would work in rows.

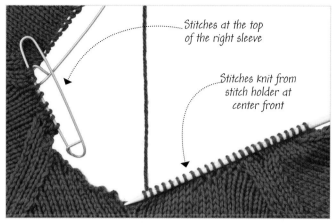

Stitches at the top of the right sleeve

Stitches knit from stitch holder at center front

Use the yarn tail to stitch the neck seam

Cast off in rib for an elastic edge

8 With all the stitches around the neck edge picked up, you can knit the neckband in double rib, to match the cuffs and hem, following the pattern instructions.

Remember After investing time and effort in knitting your sweater, make sure you sew the neckband, sleeve, and side seams neatly. Otherwise, you may ruin the finished result.

The perfect **Raglan Sweater**

The distinguishing feature of a raglan sweater is the sloping edges where the sleeves join the body of the sweater. It looks very professional, and is relatively easy to achieve.

Fully fashioned shaping
The technique of making decreases on a stocking-stitch fabric while preserving a line of stitches along each edge looks very attractive and makes sewing up a lot easier and neater.

Paired decreases
A left sloping decrease must be mirrored on the opposite edge by a right-sloping decrease. Look at the various methods for decreasing stitches shown on pp.80–83 and you will see that some

create a left slope, while some create a right slope. These characteristics are taken into account when designing the shaping on an item such as this sweater. It is important to follow the pattern instructions carefully to achieve this result.

Mattress stitch seams
There is no point in knitting fully fashioned sections for your sweater, only to ruin the effect when seaming. Instructions for sewing neat mattress stitch seams are given on p.44.

How to **Knit Cast-off Horizontal Buttonhole**

You can create a small buttonhole with a single eyelet (see pp.172–173), but to make a larger, neater buttonhole where you can alter the width of the gap to fit a specific diameter of button, use the technique shown here. Decide on the number of buttons you will be using so that you can calculate how many rows you will need to work between the buttonholes.

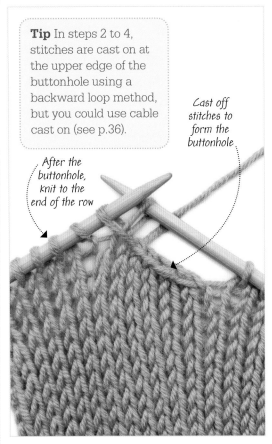

Tip In steps 2 to 4, stitches are cast on at the upper edge of the buttonhole using a backward loop method, but you could use cable cast on (see p.36).

Cast off stitches to form the buttonhole

After the buttonhole, knit to the end of the row

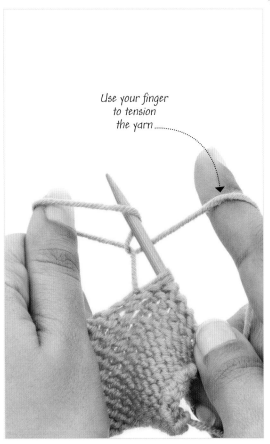

Use your finger to tension the yarn

1 On a right-side row, knit to the position of the right-hand edge of the buttonhole you want to create. Work two more stitches and pass one over the other, in a knitwise cast off (see p.42). Continue casting off enough stitches in this way, to create a gap of the desired width, then knit to the end of the row. On the next row, purl until you reach the position of the stitches you have cast off.

2 Place a point protector on the tip of the left needle to prevent stitches from slipping off, and continue using only the right needle. Hold both the yarn and the needle in your right hand and, with your left thumb pointing downward, pick up the yarn from behind and loop it around your thumb, then insert the needle into the front of this thumb loop.

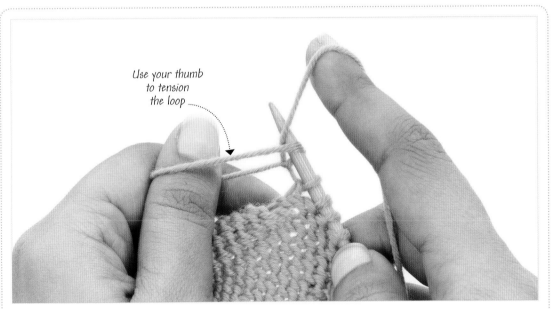

Use your thumb to tension the loop ....

3 Using your right index finger to control the yarn and your left thumb to tension the loop, wrap the yarn around the needle by bringing the yarn toward the left, behind the needle, and then back toward the right, in front of the needle.

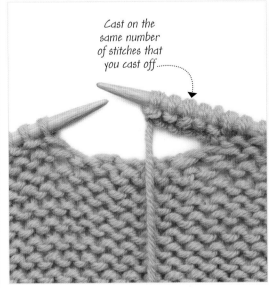

Cast on the same number of stitches that you cast off ....

4 Slip the thumb loop over the point of the needle and, holding the new loop in place with the left forefinger, use the right forefinger to tighten the loop. Repeat the process, casting on the same number of stitches that you cast off on the previous row.

Knit a Baby's Cardigan

Designed to fit a newborn and made using a soft cashmere
yarn, here is a chance to practice neckline shaping and
making a horizontal buttonhole.

Instructions

Difficulty Level
Easy

Size
To fit a newborn baby

Yarn
Rowan Pure Cashmere DK 25 g
829 Violetta x 3

Needles
1 pair of US3 (3.25 mm/UK10)
    needles

Notions
1 button
Blunt tapestry needle

Gauge
27 sts and 37 rows to 4 in (10 cm)
over st st using US3 (3.25 mm/
    UK10) needles

**829
Violetta x 3**

1 pair of US3 (3.25 mm/UK10) needles

Pattern

Using cable cast-on method (see
p.36), cast on 62 sts.
Row 1 (WS): K.
Rows 2 and 3: As row 1.
Row 4 (RS): K.
Row 5: P.
Rows 4 and 5 set st st. Continue
working in st st until work measures
6¾ in (17 cm) from cast-on edge,
ending with a WS row.

Shape Arms
Cast on 36 sts at beg of next 2
rows. (134 sts)
Starting with a k row, work in g st
for 32 rows.

Shape Right Front
Next row: K 57 and turn, leaving
rem 77 sts on a holder.

Shape Neck
Row 1: K1, s1 k1 psso, k to end.
(56 sts)

Row 2: K to last 3 sts, k2tog, k1.
(55 sts)
Row 3: As row 1. (54 sts)
Knit 11 rows without shaping,
ending with a RS row.
Inc row (WS): K1, M1, k to end.
(55 sts)
Knit 3 rows without shaping.
Cont increasing at neck edge as
set by inc row, inc on next and 3
foll alt rows, then on neck edge of
following 2 rows. (61 sts)
Next row: Cast on and k 7 sts, k
to end. (68 sts)

For a Girl Only
Place buttonhole: K to last 5 sts,
cast off 3 sts, k1.
Next row: K2, cast on 3 sts,
k to end.

For a Boy only
Knit 2 rows.

For Boy and Girl
Shape Underarm (RS): Cast off
36 sts, k to end.
Row 1 (WS): K5, p to end.
Row 2: K to end.
Rep rows 1 and 2 until work
measures 6¼ in (16 cm) from
underarm, ending with a RS row.
Knit 3 rows. Cast off.

Shape Left Front (Boy and Girl)
With RS facing, rejoin yarn to rem
sts from holder, cast off next 20 sts,
k to end. (57 sts)

Shape Neck (Boy and Girl)
Row 1 (WS): K to last 3 sts, k2tog,
k1. (56 sts)
Row 2: K1, s1 k1 psso, k to end.
(55 sts)
Row 3: As row 1. (54 sts)
Knit 12 rows without shaping,
ending with a WS row.

Inc row: K1, M1, k to end. (55sts)
Knit 2 rows without shaping.
Cont increasing at neck edge as
set by inc row, inc on next and 3
foll alt rows, then at neck edge of
following 2 rows. (61sts)
Next row (WS): K.
Next row (RS): Cast on and k
7sts, k to end. (68sts)

For a girl only
Knit 2 rows.

For a boy only
Place buttonhole: K to last 5sts,
cast off 3sts, k1.
Next row: K2, cast on 3sts,
k to end.

For a boy and girl
Shape underarm (WS): Cast off
36sts, k to end.
Row 1 (RS): K to end.

Row 2 (WS): P to last 5 sts, k5.
Rep last 2 rows until work
measures 6¼in (16 cm) from
underarm, ending with a RS row.
Knit 3 rows, cast off. Join side and
underarm seams using mattress
stitch (see p.44), Block, using the
steam blocking method (see p.141)
and attach the button.

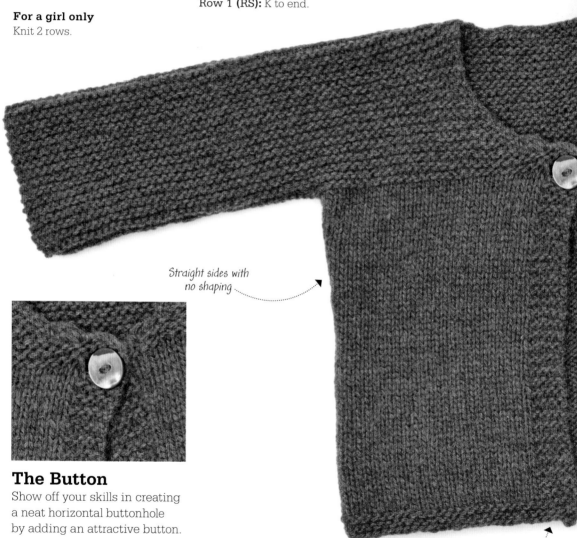

*Straight sides with
no shaping*

The Button

Show off your skills in creating
a neat horizontal buttonhole
by adding an attractive button.
Make sure that you sew
the button on securely.

Garter-stitch bands

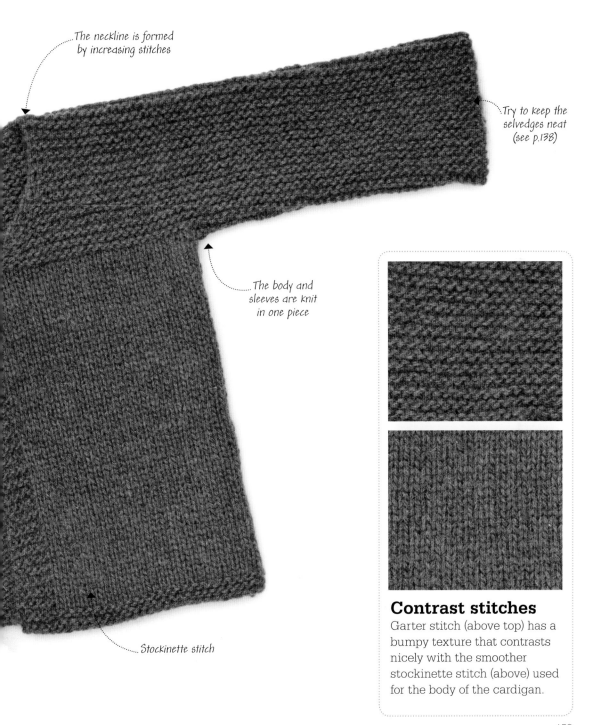

The neckline is formed
by increasing stitches

Try to keep the
selvedges neat
(see p.138)

The body and
sleeves are knit
in one piece

Stockinette stitch

Contrast stitches

Garter stitch (above top) has a
bumpy texture that contrasts
nicely with the smoother
stockinette stitch (above) used
for the body of the cardigan.

Knit a Pair of Mittens

These cozy, chunky mittens are quick to make and will
help you to learn some simple shaping techniques. You will
also use a special cast-off method at the fingertip edge,
which reduces the amount of seaming there is to do.

Instructions

Difficulty Level
Easy

Size
To fit an adult male

Yarn
Rowan Cocoon 100 g
825 Clay x 2

Needles
1 pair of US8 (5 mm/UK6) needles
1 pair of US10½ (6.5 mm/UK3)
  needles

Gauge
14 sts and 16 rows to 4 in (10 cm)
  over st st on US10½ (6.5 mm/
  UK3) needles.

Notions
Blunt tapestry needle

Special Abbreviations

s1 k1 psso

Slip 1, knit 1, pass slipped
  stitches over.

p2tog tbl

Purl 2 together through back loop.

**825
Clay x 2**

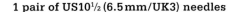

1 pair of US8 (5 mm/UK6) needles

1 pair of US10½ (6.5 mm/UK3) needles

Pattern
Right Mitten
Using US8 (5 mm/UK6) needles,
cast on 45 sts using long-tail
cast-on method (see p.38).
Row 1 (RS): K1, *p1, k1, rep from *
to end.
Row 2: P1, *k1, p1, rep from * to end.
Rep last 2 rows seven times more
(16 rows worked in total).
Change to US10½ (6.5 mm/UK3)
needles and work in st st for 4
rows.**

Shape Thumb
Row 1 (RS): K 22, M1, k4, M1, k to
end. (47 sts)
Work 3 rows without shaping.

Row 5: K 22, M1, k6, M1, k to end.
(49 sts)
Row 6: P.
Row 7: K 22, M1, k8, M1, k to end.
(51 sts)
Row 8: P.
Row 9: K 22, M1, k10, M1, k to
end. (53 sts)
Row 10: P.
Row 11: K 34 and turn, leaving
rem 19 sts on a holder.
Row 12: P 12 and turn, leaving
rem 22 sts on a holder. (12 sts)
Working only on these 12 sts, work
8 rows in st st ending with a WS
row.
Next row: *K1, k2tog, rep from *
to end. (8 sts)
Next row: P.
Next row: *K2tog, rep from * to
end. (4 sts)
Break off yarn, leaving a long tail,

and thread through rem sts.
Transfer the 19 sts from left holder
to needle, rejoin yarn and k to end.
Next row: P across 19 sts, then p
the 22 sts from rem holder. (41 sts)
Work 14 rows st st without
shaping.

Shape Top
Row 1: K2, s1 k1 psso, k 14, k2tog,
k2, s1 k1 psso, k14, k2tog, k1.
(37 sts)
Rows 2 and 4: P.
Row 3: K2, s1 k1 psso, k 12, k2tog,
k2, s1 k1 psso, k12, k2tog, k1.
(33 sts)
Row 5: K2, s1 k1 psso, k 10, k2tog,
k2, s1 k1 psso, k 10, k2tog, k1.
(29 sts)
Row 6: P1, p2tog, p 8, p2tog tbl,
p2, p2tog tbl, p 8, p2tog, p2. (25 sts)

Row 7: K2, s1 k1 psso, k6, k2tog, k2, s1 k1 psso, k6, k2tog, k1. (21sts)
Next row: P 9, p2tog, and with WS facing, cast off using three-needle cast-off method, leaving a long tail. Use long ends to sew up thumb and hand sew using mattress stitch (see p.44).

Left Mitten

Work as given for right mitten to **.

Shape Thumb

Row 1 (RS): K 19, M1, k 4, M1, k to end. (47sts)
Work 3 rows without shaping.
Row 5: K 19, M1, k 6, M1, k to end. (49sts)
Row 6: P.
Row 7: K 19, M1, k 8, M1, k to end. (51sts)
Row 8: P.
Row 9: K 19, M1, k 10, M1, k to end. (53sts)

Row 10: P.
Row 11: K 31 and turn, leaving rem 22sts on a holder.
Row 12: P 12 and turn, leaving rem 19sts on a holder. (12sts)
Complete as for right mitten.

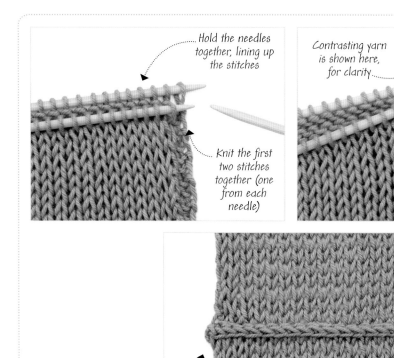

Hold the needles together, lining up the stitches

Knit the first two stitches together (one from each needle)

Contrasting yarn is shown here, for clarity

Cast off stitches in the usual way

This cast-off technique creates a neat ridge

Three-needle cast-off

Hold the needles so that the stitches to be joined sit together, with wrong sides facing each other. Insert a third needle through the loop of the first stitch on each needle and knit these two stitches together. Knit together the next two stitches from each needle; pass the first stitch on the right needle over the second, to cast it off. Continue in this way, knitting two stitches together from each needle, and casting off the resulting stitch.

Seam created by three-needle cast-off

Ribbing helps the cuff keep its elasticity

Mitten fingertips

A three-needle cast-off (see opposite) creates a neater and more comfortable finish than simply sewing a seam. Sew the side seams as usual.

Ribbed cuff

Using smaller needles for the ribbed cuffs means you can make a snug-fitting band on each mitten that keeps out the cold.

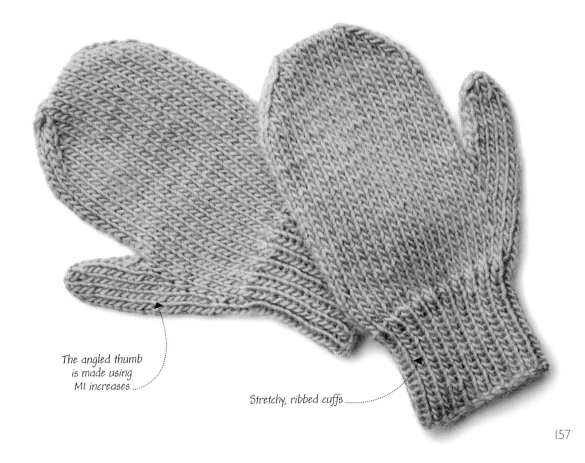

The angled thumb is made using MI increases

Stretchy, ribbed cuffs

How to **Use a Color Chart**

Charts are used for colorwork because they take up less space than pattern text, and once you understand how to read a chart you will find that they are easier to follow than written instructions. Start reading a chart from the bottom, reading odd-numbered (RS) rows from right to left, and even-numbered (WS) rows from left to right.

Intarsia chart

KEY

☐ = background color
● = motif color 1
◉ = motif color 2
☒ = motif color 3

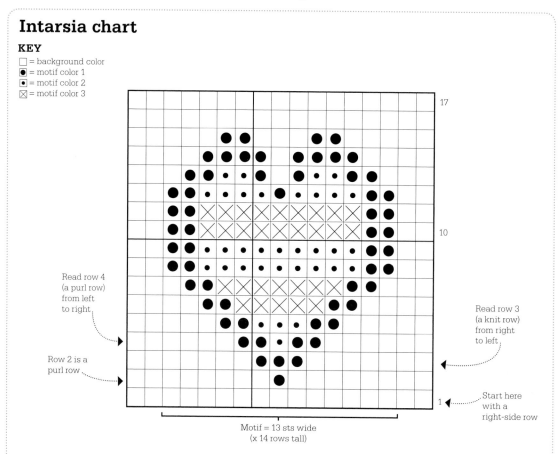

17

10

Read row 4
(a purl row)
from left
to right

Read row 3
(a knit row)
from right
to left

Row 2 is a
purl row

1

Start here
with a
right-side row

Motif = 13 sts wide
(x 14 rows tall)

Here is a simple intarsia colorwork chart for knitting a heart shape in three colors, with a fourth color used for the background. You can tell if a chart is to be worked using the intarsia technique (as opposed to Fair Isle), when a color appears only in a section of a row and not across the entire row. Each square on the chart represents a stitch, and each symbol denotes a particular color; the symbols and

their colors are listed in a separate key. When working from an intarsia chart, remember that the various colored yarns will need to be woven in on the wrong side of the work, and twisted together at color-change points to avoid creating holes. To make this process easier, and to help prevent yarns from becoming tangled, wind lengths of yarn onto bobbins (see p.23).

Fair Isle chart

KEY

☐ = background color
◉ = motif color

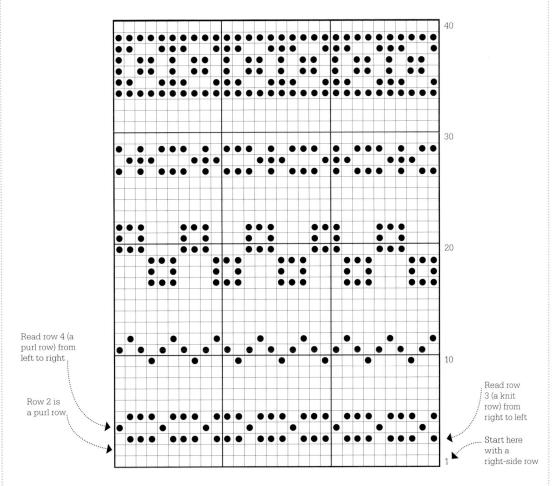

Read row 4 (a purl row) from left to right

Row 2 is a purl row

Read row 3 (a knit row) from right to left

Start here with a right-side row

In this chart, which is an example of a typical Fair Isle pattern, you will see that no more than two colors appear in any one row and the pattern extends over the entire row. Each color is used for only a few stitches at a time and the color not in use is stranded across these stitches on the wrong side of the work. As with an intarsia chart, each square represents a stitch and each symbol denotes a particular color. This chart has only one symbol for the colored squares (the "motif color") and a blank square for the background color—but this doesn't mean that you are restricted to using only two colors overall. As long as you remember to use only two colors at a time in each row, once you reach the end of a row, you can change one or both of the colors, ready for the next row.

Stitch Gallery of **Slip-Stitch Colorwork**

Slip-stitch knitting is one of the easiest methods of creating multicolored patterns. Only one color is used in each row, creating a versatile double-sided fabric. Experiment with different color combinations, since these colorful stitch patterns are an excellent way of using up scrap of yarn.

Broken Stripes

Instructions

Note: All sts to be slipped purlwise.
Using yarn A, cast on a multiple of 4sts plus 2 extra sts.
Row 1 (RS): Using yarn A, k.
Row 2: Using yarn A, p.
Rows 3 and 4: As rows 1 and 2.
Row 5: Using yarn B, k2, *s1, k3, rep from * to end.

Row 6: Using yarn B, p.
Row 7: Using yarn B, k.
Row 8: Using yarn B, p.
Row 9: Using yarn A, k4, *s1, k3, rep from * to last 2sts, s1, k1.
Rep rows 2–9 to form patt.

Weaver's Stitch

Instructions

Note: All sts to be slipped purlwise.
Using yarn A, cast on an even number of sts.
Row 1 (RS): Using yarn A, *k1, s1 wyif, rep from * to end.
Row 2: Using yarn A, *p1, s1 wyib, rep from * to end.
Row 3: Using yarn B, *k1, s1 wyif, rep from * to end.

Row 4: Using yarn B, *p1, s1 wyib, rep from * to end.
Rep rows 1–4 to form patt.

Vertical Stripes

Instructions

Note: All sts to be slipped purlwise. Gauge will be tighter as a result of slipped stitch columns, so it is advisable to cast three times as many stitches for the width.
Using yarn A, cast on a multiple of 4sts.
Row 1 (RS): Using yarn A, k.
Row 2: Using yarn A, p.
Row 3: Using yarn B, k3, s2 wyib, *k2, s2 wyib, rep from * to last 3sts, k3.

Row 4: Using yarn B, p3, s2 wyif, *p2, s2 wyif, rep from * to last 3sts, p3.
Row 5: Using yarn A, k1, s2 wyib, *k2, s2, rep from * to last st, k1.
Row 6: Using yarn A, p1, s2 wyif, *p2, s2 wyif, rep from * to last st, p1.
Rep rows 3–6 to form patt.

Honeycomb Stitch

Instructions

Note: All sts to be slipped purlwise.
Using yarn A, cast on a multiple of 4sts plus one extra st.
Row 1 (RS): Using yarn A, k.
Row 2: Using yarn A, p.
Rows 3: Using yarn B, *s1 wyib, k3, rep from * to last st, s1 wyib.
Row 4: Using yarn B, s1 wyif, *p3, s1 wyif, rep from * to last st, k1.
Row 5: Using yarn B, *s1 wyib, k3, rep from * to last st, s1 wyib.
Row 6: Using yarn B, s1 wyif, *p3, s1 wyif, rep from * to last st, k1.
Row 7: Using yarn A, k.
Row 8: Using yarn A, p.
Row 9: Using yarn C, *k2, s1 wyib, k1, rep from * to last st, k1.
Row 10: Using yarn C, p1, *p1, s1 wyif, p2, rep from * to last st, k1.
Row 11: Using yarn C, *k2, s1 wyib, k1, rep from * to last st, k1.
Row 12: Using yarn C, p1, *p1, s1 wyif, p2, rep from * to last st, k1.
Row 13: Using yarn A, k.
Row 14: Using yarn A, p.
Rep rows 3–14 to form patt.

Garter Slip Stitch

Instructions

Note: All sts to be slipped purlwise.
Using yarn C, cast on a multiple of 4sts plus 3 extra sts.
Row 1 (RS): Using yarn A, k1, *s1, k3, rep from * to last 2sts, s1, k1.
Row 2: Using yarn A, k1, *s1 wyif, k3, rep from * to last 2sts, s1 wyif, k1.
Row 3: Using yarn B, k3, *s1, k3, rep from * to end.
Row 4: Using yarn B, k3, *s1 wyif, k3, rep from * to end.
Row 5: Using yarn C, k1, *s1, k3, rep from * to last 2sts, s1, k1.
Row 6: Using yarn C, k1, *s1 wyif, k3, rep from * to last 2sts, s1 wyif, k1.
Row 7: Using yarn A, k3, *s1, k3, rep from * to end.
Row 8: Using yarn A, k3, *s1 wyif, k3, rep from * to end.
Row 9: Using yarn B, k1, *s1, k3, rep from * to last 2sts, s1, k1.
Row 10: Using yarn B, k1, *s1 wyif, k3, rep from * to last 2sts, s1 wyif, k1.
Row 11: Using yarn C, k3, *s1, k3, rep from * to end.
Row 12: Using yarn C, k3, *s1 wyif, k3, rep from * to end.
Rep rows 1–12 to form patt.

Peeping Purl Stitch

Instructions

Note: All sts to be slipped purlwise.
Using yarn A, cast on an odd number of sts.
Row 1 (RS): Using yarn A, k.
Row 2: Using yarn A, p.
Rows 3 and 4: As rows 1 and 2.
Row 5: Using yarn B, k1, *s1 wyib, k1, rep from * to end.
Row 6: Using yarn B, k1, *s1 wyif, k1, rep from * to end.
Row 7: As row 1.
Row 8: As row 2.
Rep last 2 rows once more.
Row 11: Using yarn B, s1 wyib, *k1, s1 wyib, rep from * to end.
Row 12: Using yarn B, s1 wyif, *k1, s1 wyif, rep from * to end.
Rep rows 2–12 to form patt.

Stitch Gallery of **Fair Isle Patterns**

Traditional Fair Isle patterns use only two colors in a row, with the color not being used to make a stitch carried across the back of that stitch (the wrong side of the fabric). Practice on some of the smaller border designs before moving on to the larger motifs, and have fun combining different colors.

Simple Borders

Instructions

Use the Fair Isle technique to work these border patterns. Change the background and motif colors as desired for each band of pattern.

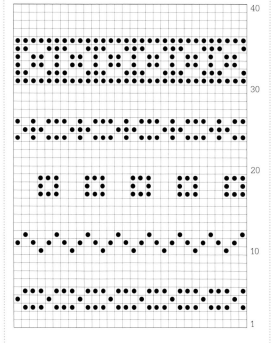

Fair Isle Blossoms

Instructions

Use the Fair Isle technique to work this repeating pattern. Choose two colors: one motif and one background. Create a multicolored effect by using a variegated yarn for the motif.

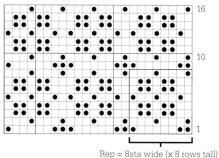

Rep = 8sts wide (x 8 rows tall)

Zigzags

Instructions

Use the three-stranded Fair Isle technique to work this repeating pattern. Choose three colors: a light, medium, and dark shade work best.

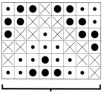

Rep = 8sts

Argyle

Instructions

Use a combination of Fair Isle methods to work this pattern. Choose three colors: one for the motif, one for the background, and one for the stripe.

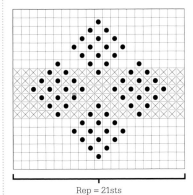

Rep = 21sts

Repeating Circles

Instructions

Use the Fair Isle technique to work this repeating pattern. Choose four colors: two motif colors and two background colors.

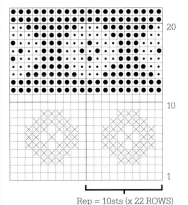

Rep = 10sts (x 22 ROWS)

Snowflake Motif

Instructions

Use either the intarsia or the Fair Isle method to work this motif. Choose two colors: one color for the motif and another for the background.

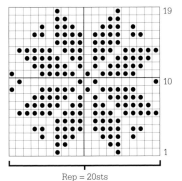

Rep = 20sts

Flower Motif

Instructions

Use the intarsia technique to work the flower motif in this pattern, unless you are repeating the pattern across the row, in which case you could use the Fair Isle technique.

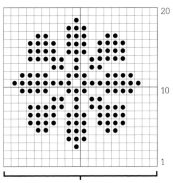

Motif = 17sts wide (x 17 rows tall)

Stitch Gallery of **Intarsia Motifs**

This technique is similar to Fair Isle, but the yarn is not stranded across
the back of the work. Intarsia is used to create larger motifs and independent
blocks of color, as well as knit "pictures." You can incorporate these designs
into areas of plain stockinette stitch fabrics or create colorful, eye-catching panels.

Heart Motif

Instructions

Use the intarsia technique to work this
heart. Choose four colors: three motif colors
and one background color.

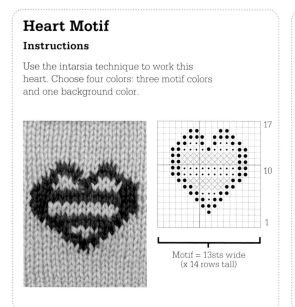

Motif = 13sts wide
(x 14 rows tall)

Climbing Vine Motif

Instructions

Use the intarsia method to work
this motif. Choose three colors:
two for the motif and one for
the background.

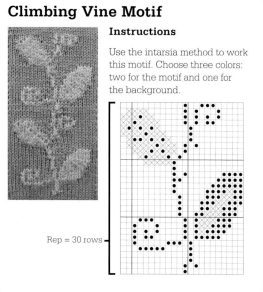

Rep = 30 rows

Duck Motif

Instructions

Use the intarsia
technique to work
this duck motif.
Choose four colors:
three colors for the
motif and one color
for the background.

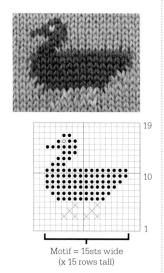

Motif = 15sts wide
(x 15 rows tall)

Pussy Cat Motif

Instructions

Use the intarsia
technique to work
this cat motif. Choose
two colors: one motif
color and one
background color.

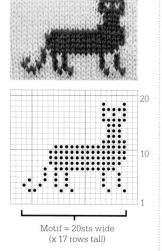

Motif = 20sts wide
(x 17 rows tall)

Bird Motif

Instructions

Use the intarsia technique to work this bird. Choose five colors: four motif colors and one background color. You could work a single motif on your knitting or arrange motifs across the knitting at random intervals or in regular repeating positions.

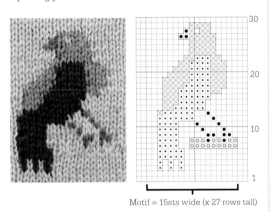

Motif = 15sts wide (x 27 rows tall)

Tulip Motif

Instructions

Use the intarsia technique to work the tulip motif and the background around the tulip head in this pattern. When working the vertical stem: be careful to twist yarns together to avoid making gaps. Choose four colors: three motif colors and one background color.

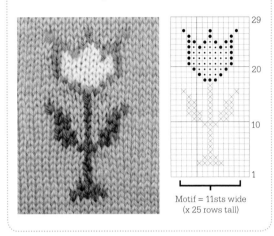

Motif = 11sts wide
(x 25 rows tall)

Little Lady Motif

Instructions

Use the intarsia technique to work this motif. Choose eight colors: seven motif colors and one background color. Work a single motif on the knitting or arrange motifs across the knitting at random intervals or in regular repeating positions.

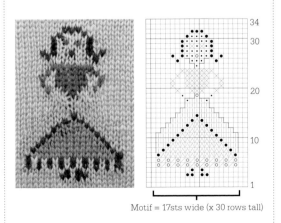

Motif = 17sts wide (x 30 rows tall)

Intarsia Flowers Motif

Instructions

Use the intarsia technique to work individual flowers or the Fair Isle technique if you are repeating them along a row. Choose four colors, two motif colors for each flower and one background color.

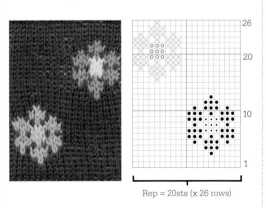

Rep = 20sts (x 26 rows)

Knit Fair Isle Arm Warmers

Gain confidence with Fair Isle colorwork by making these cozy arm warmers. The simple geometric repeat pattern is easy to work and the suggested yarns combine various fiber mixes for textural interest as well as color contrast.

Instructions

Difficulty Level
Moderate

Size
To fit an adult female

Yarn
Rowan Baby Alpaca DK 50 g
A: 216 Skipper x 1
B: 223 Electric x 1
Rowan Pure Wool DK 50 g
C: 044 Frost x 1
Rowan Cashsoft DK 50 g
D: 501 Sweet x 1

Needles
Set of four US3 (3.25 mm/UK10)
double-pointed needles
Set of four US6 (4 mm/UK8)
double-pointed needles

Notions
Blunt tapestry needle

Gauge
24 sts and 26 rows to 4 in (10 cm)
over patt, slightly stretched, on
US6 (4 mm/UK8) needles

Pattern
Left Arm Warmer
Using yarn A and US3 (3.25 mm/
UK10) needles, cast on 44 sts and
divide evenly between four needles.
Cuff round: K1, *p2, k2, rep from *
to last 3 sts, p2, k1.
Rep last round nine times more
(work 10 rounds rib in total).
Next round: Rib 4, M1, [rib 10,
M1] four times, rib to end of round.
Next round: Change to US6
(4 mm/UK8) dpns.
Working every row using the Fair
Isle method and repeating 7 sts of
chart seven times for each round,
work until arm warmer measures
7 in (18 cm) from cast-on edge,
ending with chart row 11.**

A: Skipper x 1

B: Electric x 1

C: Frost x 1

D: Sweet x 1

Set of four US3 (3.25 mm/UK10) double-pointed needles

Set of four US6 (4 mm/UK8) double-pointed needles

CHART

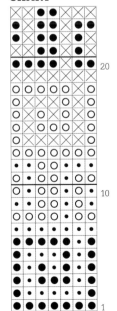

KEY

 A   B

 C   D

Thumb Opening

Next round: Work as given for chart for 9sts, cast off 6sts, patt to end of round.

Next round: Work as given for chart for 9sts, cast on 6sts, patt to end of round.

Work another 12 rows in patt as given for 7st chart repeat, ending with chart row 1.

Dec round: Using yarn A, k3, k2tog, [k7, k2tog] four times, k to end of round, at same time changing dpns to US3 (3.25m/ UK10).

Work in rib as given for cuff for 7 rounds. Cast off in rib.

Thumb

Using yarn A and US3 (3.25m/ UK10) dpns, pick up and knit 6sts from cast-off edge, pick up loop between sts and M1, then 6sts from cast-on edge of thumb opening. Pick up another loop between sts to M1. (14sts)

Thumb Round: *K1, p1, rep from * to end.

Rep last round five times.

Cast off in rib.

Darn in all ends and press lightly under a damp cloth.

Right Arm Warmer

Work as given for Left Arm warmer to **.

Thumb Opening

Next round: Work as given for chart to last 15sts, cast off 6sts, patt to end of round.

Next round: Work as given for chart for 34sts, cast on 6sts, patt to end of round.

Complete as given for Left Arm warmer.

Fair Isle Knitting

When working more than three stitches between color changes, to avoid long strands, catch it in by twisting the two yarns together at the back of the work.

Thumbs are worked by picking up stitches (see p.139)

Work the Fair Isle pattern from the chart on p.167

Ribbed cuffs are stretchy, ensuring a snug fit

When working on four needles, be careful that cast-on stitches don't become twisted

...Be careful not to cast off too tightly

Cast off loosely to create an elastic edge

Working small areas on double-pointed needles requires patience

Thumb Tube

When making the main part of the arm warmers, you will need to create a thumb hole. You must then pick up and knit 12 of the stitches around this gap, and make two extra stitches. Take your time, since this process is quite fussy.

...The thumbs, like the rest of the arm warmers, are worked on four needles

Metal needles can be heavy and tiring to work with ......

Bamboo needles are light and smooth, good for small projects like this

.... Plastic needles are an inexpensive option

Double-pointed Needles

Double-pointed needles can be challenging to work with. Practice on a small piece before starting your project, to build confidence

and understand the technique. Try needles made from different materials (see above), to judge which suits you best.

How to **Knit Lace**

The openwork texture of knited lace is formed by yarn overs and decreases, creating holes known as "eyelets." It may look complicated, but it's easier than you might think. Traditionally, knit lace was made using fine, white cotton thread, but these days there are so many interesting yarns to choose from, allowing you to be more creative.

Pseudo Lace

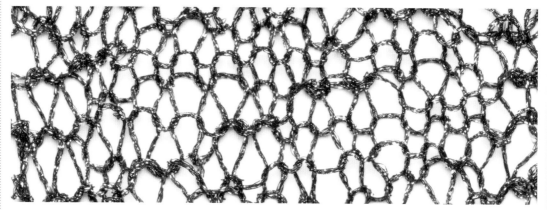

The quickest way to get a lacy effect is to knit in garter stitch—where you knit every row—but using large needles and fine yarn, so that the oversized stitches form large gaps in the fabric. Try using a metallic sock yarn with US10 (6 mm/UK4) needles for a stylish scarf.

Mohair Lace

Fine mohair yarn suits the delicacy and fragility of simple lacy patterns. It's advisable to choose a lace stitch with a simple pattern repeat because it is more challenging to knit with a fluffy yarn than a smooth one, and complicated patterns will not show up so well.

Multicolored Openwork

For added visual interest, choose a variegated yarn for a simple openwork lace pattern that has a regular, all-over repeat, such as this eyelet mesh stitch (see p.174). The color changes are more subtle than on a solid fabric, because they are broken up by the rows of holes.

Traditional-style Knited Lace

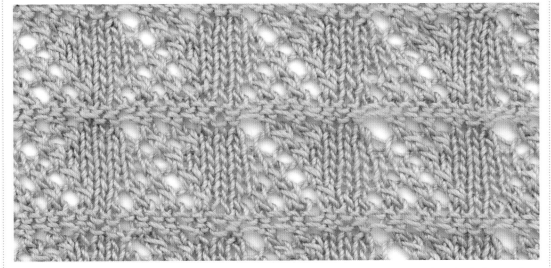

When knitting traditional lace patterns with shapes such as diamonds, leaves, and arrowheads, it is best to use a fine, smooth yarn so that the patterns of eyelet holes and solid areas can be clearly seen. The finer the yarn, the more delicate the result will be.

How to **Knit a Chain Eyelet**

Making eyelet holes is the key to creating knitted lace: the placement of
eyelets within a row is what forms the various stitch patterns, of which
there are thousands of variations. Eyelets are made from yarn overs,
which add extra stitches and are balanced by decreases, to compensate
for the increases and maintain the correct number of stitches overall.

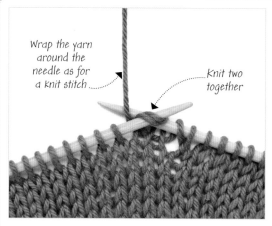

Wrap the yarn around the needle as for a knit stitch

Knit two together

1 For a chain eyelet on a stockinette-stitch
ground, begin by creating a yarn over on
the right needle (see p.76), then knit the next
two stitches together (k2tog—see p.80).

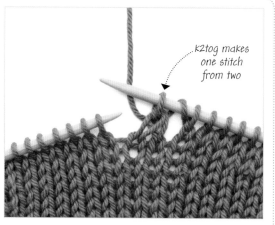

k2tog makes one stitch from two

2 The yarn over creates a hole in the fabric,
and adds an extra stitch, while the k2tog
decrease compensates for the extra stitch, so
the knitting remains the same width.

Stockinette-stitch fabric

Single chain eyelet

3 On the following row, purl the yarn over.
In addition to forming part of a lace stitch
pattern, a single chain eyelet like the one
shown here can be used for a buttonhole.

How to **Knit an Open Eyelet**

An open eyelet, like a chain eyelet, is the basic building block of most lace patterns. The technique is subtly different, and the resulting hole somewhat neater, but both methods are easy and your pattern instructions will tell you which one to use. Both the chain eyelet and the open eyelet are equally suitable for use as a small buttonhole.

...... Pass the slipped stitch over the knit stitch

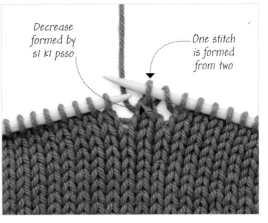

Decrease formed by s1 k1 psso

...... One stitch is formed from two

1 To make an open eyelet on a stockinette-stitch background, begin by creating a yarn over on the right needle (see p.76), then work a "s1 k1 psso" decrease (see p.82).

2 The yarn over creates a hole, and adds an extra stitch, while the s1 k1 psso decrease compensates for the extra stitch, so the knitting remains the same width.

...... Stockinette-stitch fabric

.... Single open eyelet

3 On the following row, purl the yarn over in the usual way. A single eyelet is shown here, but multiple eyelets can be arranged in various ways to create openwork patterns.

Stitch Gallery of **Lace**

Lace stitch patterns add a delicate, openwork effect in knit fabrics and are particularly appropriate for shawls, scarves, and blankets, as well as garments such as cardigans and baby clothes. The more holes in the pattern, the quicker the work grows and the less yarn needed.

Mini-leaf Stitch

Instructions

Cast on a multiple of 6sts plus 2 extra sts.
Row 1 (WS): P.
Row 2 (RS): K1, *k3, yo, s1 k2tog psso, yo, rep from * to last st, k1.
Row 3: P.
Row 4: K1, *yo, s1, k2tog psso, yo, k4, rep from * to last stis, k1.
Rep rows 1–4 to form patt.

Rep = 4 rows

Rep = 6sts

Faggoting

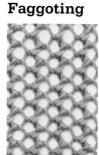

Instructions

Cast on an even number of sts.
Row 1 (RS): K1, *yo, p2tog, rep from * to last st, k1.
Row 2: As row 1.
Rep rows 1 and 2 to form patt.

Vertical Mesh Stitch

Instructions

Cast on an odd number of sts.
Row 1: K1, *yo, k2tog, rep from * to end.
Row 2: P.
Row 3: *Ssk, yo, rep from * to last st, k1.
Row 4: P.
Rep rows 1–4 to form patt.

Eyelet Mesh Stitch

Instructions

Cast on a multiple of 3sts.
Row 1 (RS): K2, *k2tog, yo, k1, rep from * to last st, k1.
Row 2: P.
Row 3: K2, *yo, k1, k2tog, rep from * to last st, k1.
Row 4: P.
Rep rows 1–4 to form patt.

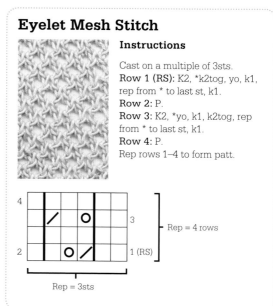

Rep = 4 rows

Rep = 3sts

Openwork Diamonds

Instructions

Cast on a multiple of 12sts plus 7 extra sts.

Row 1 (RS): *K2, k2tog, yo, k8, rep from * to last 7sts, k2, k2tog, yo, k3.

Row 2 and all foll alt rows: P.

Row 3: *K1, k2tog, yo, k2tog, yo, k7, rep from * to last 7sts, k1, k2tog, yo, k2tog, yo, k2.

Row 5: As row 1.

Row 7: K.

Row 9: *K8, k2tog, yo, k2, rep from * to last 7sts, k7.

Row 11: *K7, k2tog, yo, k2tog, yo, k1, rep from * to last 7sts, k7.

Row 13: As row 9.

Row 15: K.

Row 16: P.

Rep these 16 rows to form patt.

Leaf Eyelet Pattern

Instructions

Cast on a multiple of 8sts plus 7 extra sts.

Row 1 (RS): K.

Row 2 and all even-numbered (WS) rows: P.

Row 3: K1, *yo, s1 k2tog psso, yo, k5, rep from * to last 5 sts, yo, s1 k2tog psso, yo, k1.

Row 5: K1, *k1, yo, ssk, k5, rep from * to last 4sts, k1, yo, ssk, k1.

Row 7: K.

Row 9: K1, *k4, yo, s1 k2tog psso, yo, k1, rep from * to last 5sts, k4.

Row 11: K1, *k5, yo, ssk, k1, rep from * to last 4 sts, k4.

Row 12: P.

Rep rows 1–12 to form patt.

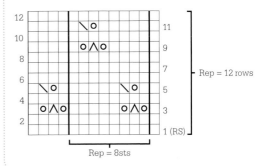

Big Leaf Lace

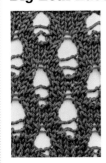

Instructions

Cast on a multiple of 8sts plus 2 extra sts.

Row 1 (RS): K3, *k2tog, yo twice, ssk, k4, rep from * to last 7sts, k2tog, yo twice, ssk, k3.

Row 2 and all even-numbered (WS) rows: P, working [k1, p1] into every double yo and p1 into single yo at beg and end of row.

Row 3: K2, *k2tog, k1, yo twice, k1, ssk, k2, rep from *.

Row 5: K1, *k2tog, k2, yo twice, k2, ssk, rep from * to last st, k1.

Row 7: K1, y9o, *ssk, k4, k2tog, yo twice, rep from * to last 9sts, ssk, k4, k2tog, yo, k1.

Row 9: K1, yo, *k1, ssk, k2, k2tog, k1, yo twice, rep from * to last 9sts, k1, ssk, k2, k2tog, k1, yo, k1.

Row 11: K1, yo, *k2, ssk, k2tog, k2, yo twice, rep from * to last 9sts, k2, ssk, k2tog, k2, yo, k1.

Row 12: Rep row 2.

Rep rows 1–12 to form patt.

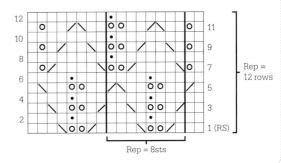

Star Eyelet Stitch

Instructions
Special abbreviations

s2 k1 p2sso: Slip 2sts, knit 1st, pass 2 slipped sts over.

Cast on a multiple of 8sts plus 5 extra sts.
Row 1 (RS): K4, *ssk, yo, k1, yo, k2tog, k3, rep from * to last st, k1.
Row 2 and all even-numbered (WS) rows: P.
Row 3: K5, *yo, s2 k1 p2sso, yo, k5, rep from * to end.
Row 5: Rep row 1.
Row 7: Ssk, yo, k1, yo, k2tog, *k3, ssk, yo, k1, yo, k2tog, rep from * to end.
Row 9: K1, *yo, s2 k1 p2sso, yo, k5, rep from *, ending last rep k1 (instead of k5).
Row 11: Rep row 7.
Row 12: P.
Rep rows 1–12 to form patt.

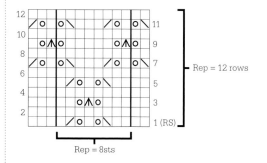

Rep = 8sts

Leaves Lace

Instructions

Cast on a multiple of 6sts plus one extra st.
Row 1 (RS): K1, *yo, ssk, k1, k2tog, yo, k1, rep from * to end.
Row 2: P.
Rows 3–6: [Rep rows 1 and 2] twice.
Row 7: K2, *yo, s1 k2tog psso, yo, k3, rep from *, ending last rep k2 (instead of k3).
Row 8 and all foll even-numbered (WS) rows: P.
Row 9: K1, *k2tog, yo, k1, yo, ssk, k1, rep from * to end.
Row 11: K2tog, *yo, k3, yo, s1 k2tog psso, rep from * to last 5sts, yo, k3, yo, ssk.
Row 12: P.
Rep rows 1–12 to form patt.

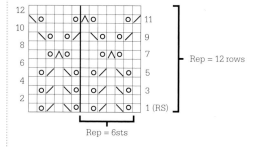

Rep = 12 rows

Rep = 6sts

Victory Lace

Instructions

Cast on a multiple of 8sts plus 6 extra sts.
Row 1: K5, *s1 k1 psso, yo, k6, rep from * to last st, k1.
Row 2 and all foll alt rows: P.
Row 3: K4, *s1 k1 psso, yo, k1, yo, k2tog, k3, rep from * to last st, k1.
Row 5: K3, *s1 k1 psso, yo, k3, yo, k2tog, k1, rep from * to last st, k1.
Row 7: K.

Row 8: P.
Rep rows 1–8 to form patt.

Arrowhead Lace

Instructions

Cast on a multiple of 8sts plus 5 extra sts.

Row 1 (RS): K1, *yo, s1 k2tog psso, yo, k5, rep from * to last 4sts, yo, s1 k2tog psso, yo, k1.

Row 2 and all even-numbered (WS) rows: P.

Row 3: Rep row 1.

Row 5: K4, *yo, ssk, k1, k2tog, yo, k3, rep from * to last st, k1.

Row 7: K1, *yo, s1 k2tog psso, yo, k1, rep from *.

Row 8: P.

Rep rows 1–8 to form patt.

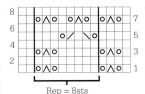

Diamond Lace Stitch

Instructions

Cast on a multiple of 10sts plus one extra st.

Row 1 (RS): K1, *k1, k2tog, [k1, yo] twice, k1, ssk, k2, rep from * to end.

Row 2 and all even-numbered (WS) rows: P.

Row 3: K1, *k2tog, k1, yo, k3, yo, k1, ssk, k1, rep from * to end.

Row 5: K2tog, *k1, yo, k5, yo, k1, s1 k2tog psso, rep from *, ending last rep ssk (instead of s1 k2tog psso).

Row 7: K1, *yo, k1, ssk, k3, k2tog, k1, yo, k1, rep from * to end.

Row 9: K1, *k1, yo, k1, ssk, k1, k2tog, k1, yo, k2, rep from * to end.

Row 11: K1, *k2, yo, k1, s1 k2tog psso, k1, yo, k3, rep from * to end.

Row 12: P.

Rep rows 1–12 to form patt.

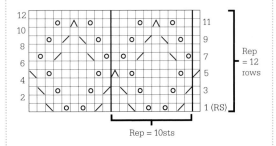

Zigzag Mesh Stitch

Instructions

Cast on a multiple of 10sts plus one extra st.

Row 1 (RS): K1, *[yo, ssk] twice, k1, [k2tog, yo] twice, k1, rep from * to end.

Row 2: P.

Row 3: K1, *k1, yo, ssk, yo, s1 k2tog psso, yo, k2tog, yo, k2, rep from * to end.

Row 4: P.

Rep rows 1–4 to form patt.

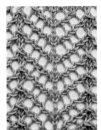

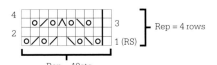

Ladder Lace

Instructions

Cast on a multiple of 6sts plus 3 extra sts.
Row 1 (RS): K3, *yo, s1k, k2tog, psso, yo, k3, rep from * to end.
Row 2: P.
Rep rows 1 and 2 to form patt.

Eyelet Lines

Instructions

Cast on a multiple of 2sts.
Row 1 (RS): K.
Row 2 and all foll alt rows: P.
Row 3: As row 1.
Row 5: K1, *k2tog, yo, rep from * to last st, k1.
Row 6: P.
Rep rows 1–6 to form patt.

Lace Openwork

Instructions

Cast on any number of sts.
Row 1 (WS): P.
Row 2: K.
Row 3: P.
Row 4: *Insert RH needle into next st as
if to knit, wrap yarn around RH needle three times and
bring all 3 loops through this st, rep from * to end.
Row 5: *Purl next st in first of the 3 loops only, allowing
remaining 2 loops in this st to fall off LH needle and extend
to full length, rep from * to end.
Rep rows 2–5 to form patt.

Horseshoe Lace

Instructions

Cast on a multiple of 10sts plus one extra st.

Row 1 (RS): K1, *yo, k3, s1 k2tog psso, k3, yo, k1, rep from * to end.

Row 2 and all foll alt rows: P.

Row 3: K2, *yo, k2, s1 k2tog psso, k2, yo, k3, rep from * to last 9sts, yo, k2, s1 k2tog psso, k2, yo, k2.

Row 5: K3, *yo, k1, s1 k2tog psso, k1, yo, k5, rep from * to last 8sts, yo, k1, s1 k2tog psso, k1, yo, k3.

Row 7: K4, *yo, s1 k2tog psso, yo, k7, rep from * to last 7sts, yo, s1 k2tog psso, yo, k4.

Row 8: P.

Rep rows 1–8 to form patt.

Godmother's Edging

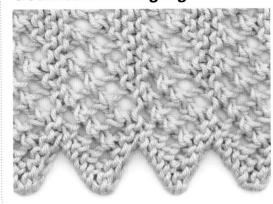

Instructions

Note: Slip first st of even-numbered rows purlwise, then take yarn to back of work between two needles ready to k next st.

Cast on 15sts.

Row 1 (RS): K.

Row 2: S1, k2, [yo, k2tog] five times, yo, k2. (16sts)

Row 3 and all odd-numbered (RS) rows: K.

Row 4: S1, k5, [yo, k2tog] four times, yo, k2. (17sts)

Row 6: S1, k8, [yo, k2tog] three times, yo, k2. (18sts)

Row 8: S1, k11, [yo, k2tog] twice, yo, k2. (19sts)

Row 10: S1, k18.

Rows 11: Cast off 4sts knitwise, k to end. (15sts)

Rep rows 2–11 until edging is desired length, ending with a row 11.

Cast off knitwise.

Christening Edging

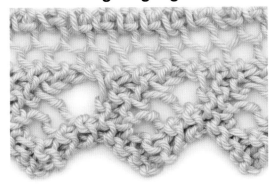

Instructions

Cast on 7sts.

Row 1 (RS): K2, yo, k2tog, yo twice, k2tog, k1. (8sts)

Row 2: K3, p1, k2, yo, k2tog.

Row 3: K2, yo, k2tog, k1, yo twice, k2tog, k1. (9sts)

Row 4: K3, p1, k3, yo, k2tog.

Row 5: K2, yo, k2tog, k2, yo twice, k2tog, k1. (10sts)

Row 6: K3, p1, k4, yo, k2tog.

Row 7: K2, yo, k2tog, k6.

Row 8: Cast off 3sts knitwise, k4, yo, k2tog. (7sts)

Rep rows 1–8 until edging is desired length, ending with a row 8.

Cast off knitwise.

Knit a Peekaboo Lace Scarf

Improve your knitting skills with an ingenious stitch: it involves knitting into a stitch worked three rows below so you can tug gathered loops of yarn into a cluster. Using two balls of luxury yarn, this scarf is 40 in (100 cm) long—but if you want yours to be longer, just keep going until the yarn runs out.

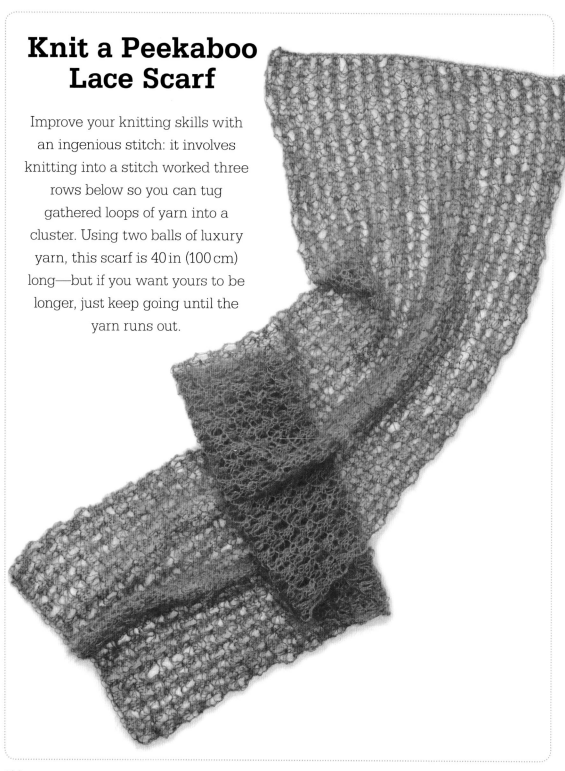

Instructions

Difficulty Level
Difficult

Size
40 x 11 in (100 x 28 cm)

Yarn
Rowan Kidsilk Haze 25 g
596 Marmalade x 2

Needles
1 pair of US7 (4.5 mm/UK7)
needles

Notions
Blunt tapestry needle

Gauge
15 sts and 16 rows to 4 in (10 cm)
measured over pattern using US7
(4.5 mm/UK7) needles

Special Abbreviations
k1b3 Knit one three rows below:
insert the tip of the needle not
into the next stitch, but into the
corresponding stitch three rows
below, allowing the stitches above
to come undone.

**596
Marmalade x 2**

1 pair of US7 (4.5 mm/UK7) needles

Pattern
Note: When dropping yarnovers
from needle, please be aware that
this refers to the yo worked on the
previous row: it will therefore
present on the left-hand needle.
You may have to tease yarn into
shape after rows 5 and 9.

Cast on 42 sts using knit-on cast-on
method (see p.34).
Row 1 (RS): K.
Row 2 (WS): K1, yo, p1, yo, *p1,
k1, p1, yo, p1, yo, rep from * to last
5 sts, p1, k1, p1, yo, p1, yo, k1.
(65 sts)
Row 3: K1, *drop next yo off LH

needle, yo, k1, drop next yo off LH
needle, yo, k3, rep from * to last
4 sts, drop next yo off LH needle,
yo, k1, drop next yo off LH needle,
yo, k1. (65 sts)
Row 4: K1, drop next yo off LH
needle, yo, p1, drop next yo off LH
needle, yo, *p3, drop next yo off LH
needle, p1, drop next yo off LH
needle, yo, rep from * to last 5 sts,
p3, drop next yo off LH needle, p1,
drop next yo off LH needle, yo, k1.
(65 sts)
Row 5: Dropping all yos from
previous row, k1, *yo, k1b3, yo,
p3tog tbl, rep from * to last 2 sts,
yo, k1b3, yo, k1. (46 sts)
Row 6: K1, p1, k1, p1, *yo, p1, yo,
p1, k1, p1, rep from * to last st, k1.

(65 sts)
Row 7: K1, *k3, drop next yo off
LH needle, yo, k1, drop next yo off
LH needle, yo, rep from * to last
4 sts, k4. (65 sts)
Row 8: Dropping all yos from
previous row, k1, *p3, drop next yo
off LH needle, yo, p1, drop next yo
off LH needle, yo, p3, rep from * to
last st, k1. (65 sts)
Row 9: K1, *p3tog tbl, yo, k1b3,
yo, rep from * to last 4 sts, p3tog
tbl, k1. (43 sts)
Rows 2 to 9 set patt. Cont until
work measures 40 in (100 cm),
or desired length, ending with
a WS row.
Next row: K.
Cast off. Darn in ends.

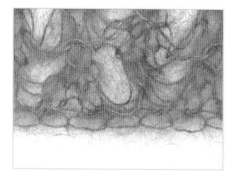

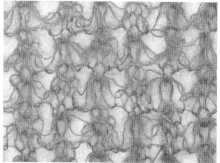

Lace cast on

To cast on, use the knit-on cast-on method (pp.34–35), which is flexible and blends in well with the knit lace fabric.

Lace-mesh pattern

A special stitch sequence (k1b3) is used to create evenly-spaced clusters of stitch loops, interspersed with holes, for the lacy effect.

The stitch pattern combines clusters of stitches with evenly spaced holes

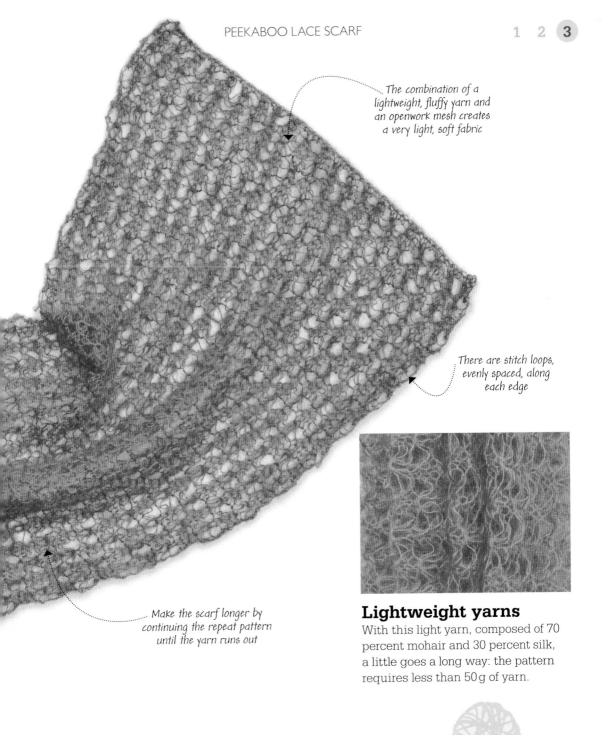

The combination of a lightweight, fluffy yarn and an openwork mesh creates a very light, soft fabric

There are stitch loops, evenly spaced, along each edge

Make the scarf longer by continuing the repeat pattern until the yarn runs out

Lightweight yarns

With this light yarn, composed of 70 percent mohair and 30 percent silk, a little goes a long way: the pattern requires less than 50 g of yarn.

Also learn to make ▶ ▶ ▶

Queen of Heart Socks

These socks are knit in the round using four double-pointed needles. Starting with the ribbed cuff at the top and ending at the toe, the lace pattern is worked in reverse, with the heart motifs appearing upside down as you knit. You will be practicing yarn-over and decreasing techniques and short-row shaping to "turn" the heel.

Instructions

Difficulty Level

Moderate

Size

To fit an adult female, shoe size US 4–10 (UK 5–8)

Yarn

Lionbrand Sock-Ease(™) 100 g
Lollipop x 1

Needles

1 pair of 3 mm (US n/a/UK11) double-pointed needles

Gauge

30 sts and 37 rows to 4 in (10 cm) over st st using 3 mm (US n/a/ UK11) double-pointed needles

Special Abbreviations

S1p Slip one stitch purlwise

Pattern

(Make 2)

Cast on 60 sts using long-tail cast-on method (see pp.38–39), and join to form a round.

Ribbed Cuff Round

The top of a sock needs to be stretchy, to grip the shin, so the socks stay up. This ribbing starts off with slightly fewer stitches than the rest of the leg, to help ensure a good fit.
 *K1, p1, rep from * to end of round.
Rep cuff round 18 more times (19 rounds worked in total).

Increase for sock: [Rib 15, M1] four times. (64 sts) Work 2 rounds k.

Place Chart

For every following round, work as given for 32 sts of chart twice. Remember that working in the round, you will only ever in this instance read the chart from right to left. Continue working in chart until work measures 7 in (18 cm), or desired length to heel shaping, ending after chart row 12 or 26.

Divide for Heel

Next row: K16, turn. S1, p31 onto same needle. These set 32 heel sts. Rearrange sts so that 32 sts sit on one needle for heel, and remaining 32 sts are divided across two needles, unworked.

Heel

Next row: S1, k31.
Next row: S1, p31.
Rep last 2 rows 11 times more (22 rows worked in total for heel flap).

Turn Heel

Next row: S1, k21, s1 k1 psso, k1.
Next row: S1, p13, p2tog, p1, turn.
Next row: S1, k14, s1 k1 psso, k1, turn.
Next row: S1, p15, p2og, p1, turn.
Cont working short-row shaping in this way, bringing an extra stitch into heel shaping, finishing with the following rows:
Next row: S1, k20, s1 k1 psso, turn.
Next row: S1, p21, p2tog, turn. 22 live sts remain.

Rejoin Round

Next round: S1, k21, pick up and k 15 sts along side of heel, work next 32 sts as given in chart, pick up and k15 from other side of heel flap, k11. This point marks end of round. Rearrange sts so that 26 sts are on needles 1 and 3, 32 patt instep sts on needle 2.
Next round: K.
Next round: K to last 3 sts on needle 1, k2tog, k1. Work as given in chart across 32 instep sts. On needle 3, k1, s1 k1 psso, and k to end. Rep last round until 64 sts remain.

Cont working in st st for underside of heel and in chart patt on instep until work measures 6¾in (17 cm) from start of heel shaping, ending with all-knit row.

Shape Toe
Next row: K.
Toe-shaping round: K to last 3sts on needle 1, k2tog, k1. Work as given for chart across 32 instep sts. On needle 3, k1, s1 k1 psso, and k to end.
Work 2 rounds without shaping.
Decreasing as set by toe-shaping round, dec on next round, foll alt round, and then every foll round until 16sts remain in total. Turn sock inside out through middle of dpns, p4, and then cast off using the three-needle cast-off method (see p.156). Darn in ends and block if desired.
Work second sock.

.... *Lacy hearts are worked "upside down"*

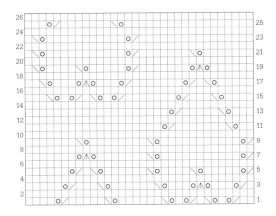

.... *Shape the heel with short rows*

Using a chart
Many sock patterns start at the top and work from the cuff toward the toe. When you incorporate a pattern from a chart into your sock, you have to invert it, working from the top of the chart to the bottom, so the motifs are the right way up.

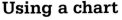

KEY

▢ k on RS rows, p on WS

⟋ k2tog

Ⓞ yon

⟍ ssk

⟑ s2 k1 p2sso

Careful! Follow the pattern carefully when shaping the heel—a loose gauge may cause gaps in the heel flap. Knit through the back of each stitch loop for the first round after picking up the stitches to twist the stitches and help to prevent any holes.

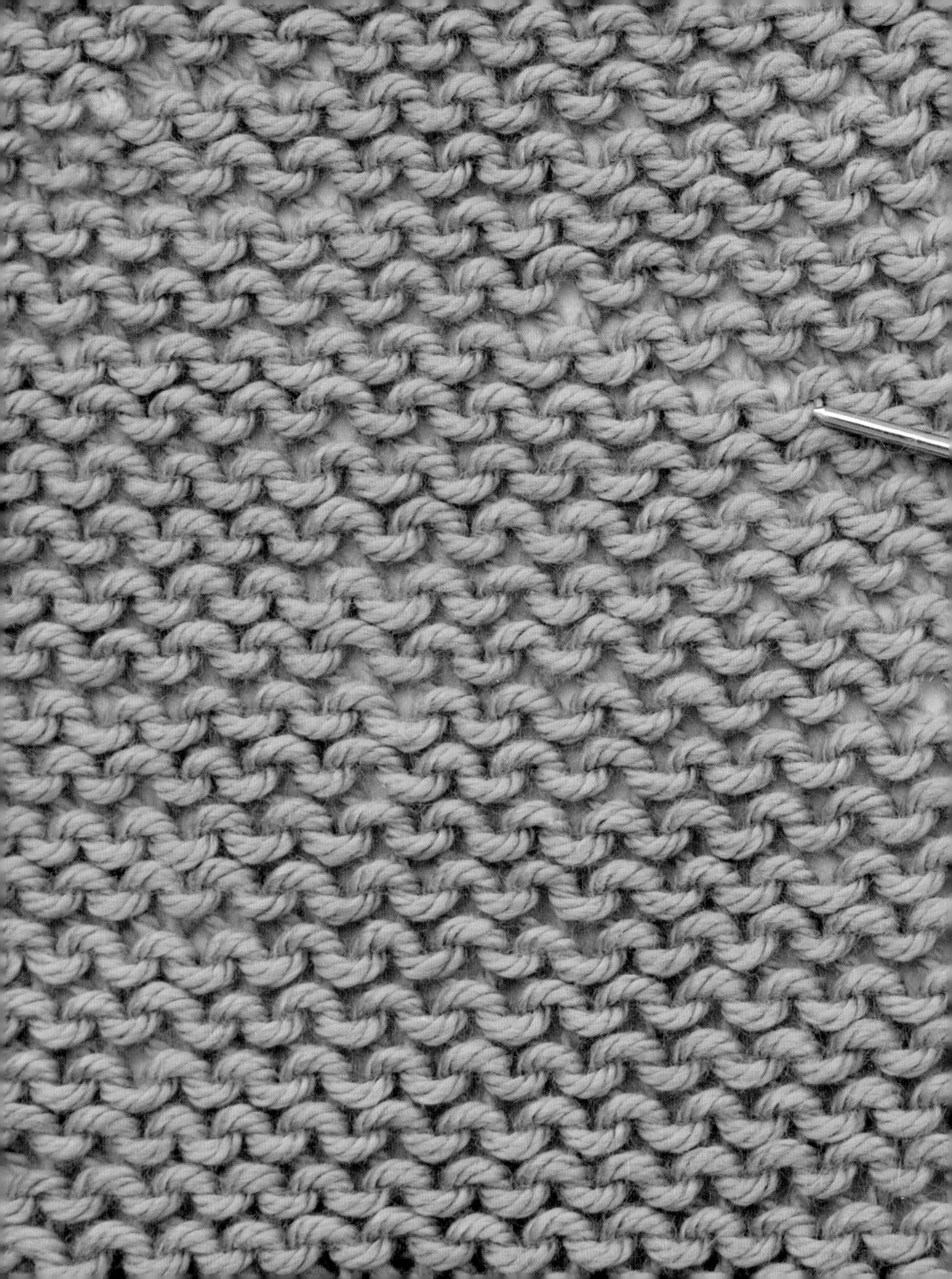

Index

About the Author

Susie Johns studied Fine Art at the Slade School in London, before working as a magazine and partworks editor for 11 years, specializing in cookery and crafts. She has written and illustrated books on a variety of creative subjects, including knitting, crochet, embroidery, and papercrafts, and has had features and interviews published in a wide range of magazines.

As a knitting designer, Susie's creative skills are in great demand, not only for making garments and accessories but also novelty knits such as fruits, vegetables, flowers, animals, birds, dolls, mascots, and puppets.

Susie teaches drawing and painting at an adult education college in Greenwich, London, and runs workshops in knitting, crochet, and customizing clothes. She is the founder member of "Knitting Night at The Pelton", a weekly drop-in group.

Acknowledgments

Photographic Credits

The publishers would like to thank **Andy Crawford** and **Dave King** for new photography.
All images © Dorling Kindersley.
For further information see
www.dkimages.com

Author Acknowledgments

I would like to thank Annelise Evans for her dedication and editorial input and the team at DK who worked so hard to make this book possible—in particular Becky Shackleton, Gemma Fletcher, Alastair Laing, and Helen Fewster.

Publisher's Acknowledgments

Many people helped in the making of this book. Special thanks are due to **Linda Bingham**, who designed and made up the projects featured on pp.46–51. Dorling Kindersley would also like to thank:

In the UK
Design assistance Sunita Gahir, Leah Germann, Vicky Read
Editorial assistance Annelise Evans
DK Images Claire Bowers, Freddie Marriage, Emma Shepherd, Romaine Werblow
Indexer Chris Bernstein

At Tall Tree Ltd
Editor Joe Fullman
Designer Jonathan Vipond

In India
Senior Editor Garima Sharma
Design assistance Karan Chaudhary, Era Chawla, Devan Das, Prashant Kumar, Ankita Mukherjee, Pooja Verma
Editorial assistance Arani Sinha